MEGA MORTGAGES

Money Making Manual

The Complete Course in Investing in Notes, Mortgages and Cash Flows

By E. Wright Davis, JD

Copyright © 2011 E. Wright Davis

Mega Mortgages

Table of Contents

Table of Contents...Continued

Table of Contents...Continued

Table of Contents...Continued

Illustrations **(Following Page 166)**

Free purchase quotation for note holders

Cash flows you might not know about

Request for quote- Seasoned First Note

Request for quote- Simultaneous Closing

Existing Note Work Sheet

Note Purchase Data Sheet

Agreement to Broker Instrument(s) known as

Table of Contents...Continued

About the Author/Instructor

E. Wright Davis

A member of the State Bar of Georgia for over 40 years, a trial lawyer, mortgage broker, real estate investor, realtor and title insurance company president.

The author and creator of five real estate investment courses and has developed an online real estate law course for a major university.

As a state supreme court certified mediator in two states, he understands real estate dispute resolution and foreclosure resolution.

Is the author of four books; *Legal Vengeance* (fiction), *Mega Mortgages, How to Crack the Mortgage Code* and *Getting Started in Creative Real Estate Investing.*

For ten years he was a state licensed real estate salesperson and real estate broker instructor.

Served as a Delegate to the U.S.–China Conference on Trade Investment and Economic Law in Beijing China and was selected as One of Five Outstanding Men of Georgia by the Georgia Jaycees.

www.megamortgages.ewrightdavis.com

Acknowledgements

I wish to express my deepest gratitude to the following people who helped make this book possible:

To Gail White of Tailored PC Documents, to whom I am greatly appreciative for her word processing, organizational and publishing skills. (www.tailoredpcdocuments.biz)

And to my wife, Cynthia, whose talent and computer skills made this book come together.

And my students who have taken my investing courses, Crack the Mortgage Code, Calculator Power, Getting Started in Creative Real Estate Investing, and my students in the real estate salesman and mortgage broker licensing courses throughout the years who gave me the inspiration and ideas for this book.

www.megamortgages.ewrightdavis.com

Paper vs. Real Estate: No Contest!

By John Behle

"OUCH! Honey, I got another paper cut. Can we buy an electric envelope opener?

Also, please pick up some more deposit slips when you are out and some Grey Poupon."

Sure beats Landlordingl

I remember the days of being a landlord (*though a therapist would probably tell me to try forget*). Plunging toilets and chasing tenants around trying to get rent never was fun for me. Calls at 3:00 in the morning over leaky taps may be an exciting challenge for some people. A tenant rebuilding a Harley Davidson on the living room carpet might be no big deal for a tough, macho, hardened landlord, but I'd rather invest safer and more profitably.

No More 3:00 a.m. Calls!

I've never had a mortgage call me at 3:00 in the morning. I've never had a mortgage get in a fight with the mortgage upstairs. Mortgages don't lie to me. Mortgages don't drive away in pickup trucks owing me money.

Loan-lording is Safer!

With a tenant, you have no collateral for what they owe you. You are effectively loaning money to someone specifically because they can't afford it. With a mortgage, you have their money as collateral and they have a strong interest in paying you.

Better Than Triple-Net!

A tenant is not an owner. Much of the time, pride of ownership is lacking and they can beat a property to pieces. You are responsible for all major and minor repairs.

An owner is responsible for all repairs and problems. The lender has a set payment and costs.

Price/Rent Depreciating

In an economic decline, a landlord's equity can be wiped out with a 20% drop in prices. The lender's equity takes priority. The fair market rent can go down. Payments on mortgages are fixed.

Yield Appreciation

Sure, in an appreciating market, real estate values can go up. I'll never be the one to say it never makes sense to own real estate. But... Mortgages can appreciate too.

When properties go up in value, refinancing increases. As that happens, *payers are chasing you down and paying you off* at full face value on notes.

That means that a $10,000 note that I might buy for $8,000 can end up paying off overnight for the full $10,000. A $100,000 mortgage bought for $75,000 pays off for a $25,000 profit.

I call that appreciation, I appreciate it ever time it happens. It can happen in down markets too.

Also, when rents and values are going up, it is a good time to trigger some additional payments on the principal of the loan. I encourage payers to pay extra principal payments to pay the loan off much earlier and save thousands in interest.

When a payer on a note increases his payment, my yield may double. By the way, there are over a hundred ways to improve profits on notes. They work in up, down, or any market. The leverage possibilities with notes equal or exceed any other form of investment. It is not only possible, but also simple to invest in notes with 100% or more financing.

A Free Note!

Using both private and institutional sources, I have routinely financed notes for more than the cost of my purchase. This would he a risky procedure in real estate, but not in notes.

I can finance a note 100% and have a cash flow when I am done. I can finance notes for as much as 200% of the cost of purchase and still have a cash flow in some cases.

Here's a recent example from one of my students: A property sold for $52,000 with $12,000 down. The $40,000 note was paid on for seven years and then went into default.

The note was purchased for $10,000 and restructured to $44,000 at 10% with a payment of $424.61 for 240 months, An investor loaned $52,.000 against the note at 12 percent with a payment of $220.22 per month.

My student put almost $10,000 cash in his pocket and has a cash flow of over $200 per month for the next 20 years.

Most real estate investors take leverage for granted and don't realize it is just as powerful when applied to other investments.

No Tax Advantages?

Could a totally tax-free investment that doesn't cost anything be considered a tax advantage?

IRAs and pension funds can invest in notes. You could be receiving 14% or more interest and a compounding cash flow in your IRA. You can even buy and sell notes in your IRA. Let's look at an example of how to put $80,000 into an IRA for free.

Notes sell at a discount. If I bought a $50,000 note at a 16% yield, it would look like this:

$50,000 @ 10%
$438.79 for 360 months

My cost:
$32,630 @ 16%
$438.79 for 360 months

If I purchased this note in an IRA and then sold off half of it at a 14% yield, I would receive the following:

$32,949 @ 14%
$438.79 for 180 months

This would leave me with $319 more than it cost to buy the whole note and then payments of $438.79 per month for 15 years that begin in 15 years.

That totals over $80,000 in profit that didn't cost a cent and is tax-deferred until retirement.

I'm not saying "don't invest in real estate." I only suggest that paper stacks up as well or better than most real estate.

Fewer Problems

Many of the standard problems real estate investors run into, like property management, low cash flows, balloon payments and market price fluctuations, are avoided or minimized by paper investment.

Retirement or financial independence can be summarized in two words: "Cash Flow."

Why invest time and energy in an investment that may take many years to create a safe cash flow when you could begin investing in the purchase of cash flows by buying paper?

Immediate cash flows that increase over time with little management! There is no need to wait 10 to 20 years to see equity and cash flow from your efforts.

Notes:

_____

_____

_____

_____

_____

_____

_____

_____

Basics of Seller Carry-back Notes.

Whenever any person, partnership. trust, corporation or any other entity becomes a lender on a parcel of real property, a promissory note is created. You became the lender when you sold your real estate and carried back a note.

The Promissory Note

A promissory note is a written promise to pay a certain amount of money, and its payment is secured by some type of security instrument that becomes a lien on the real property.

The elements of a note include:

(1) the amount of the loan (principal);

(2) the interest rate (interest);

(3) the amount and frequency of payments (debt service);

(4) when the borrower must repay the principal (due date); and

(5) the penalties imposed if borrower fails to timely pay or tender a payment (late charge) or decides to pay a portion or all of the principal prior to the due date (pre-payment penalty), The promissory note identifies the person who makes the payments to you (the buyer of your property—the borrower-mortgagor) and the person who receives the payments (you)-mortgagee.

The Security instrument

The security instrument is the document that provides for the alternate repayment of the debt to you in the case of default by the borrower. The security instrument is recorded in the county recorder's office as a lien against the title of the property you sold.

There are three kinds of instruments used to make real estate security for a debt:

(1) mortgage, with or without the power of sale;

(2) deed of trust; and

(3) land contract, The land contract—known by many names such as installment contract, contract for deed, contract of sale, conditional sales contract, and the like—is used on occasion. However, a discussion of mortgages helps with the understanding of other security devices. State law prescribes what type of security instrument is used in that state.

Mortgage

The mortgage gives the lender a lien on the real estate and pledges it as security for the note. The borrower, who is the buyer of the property, is called the *mortgagor*. The lender is called the mortgagee.

If the borrower does not pay, the lender may go to court through a procedure called a *judicial foreclosure*, that is, foreclosure through the courts, In this procedure, he has the court sell the property and, out of the money obtained from the sale, take enough to pay the expenses of the foreclosure and pay off the debt.

Deed of Trust

When a *deed of trust* is used, an additional party called a *trustee* is brought into the transaction. The borrower, called the *trustor*, transfers "bare legal title" but nothing more to the trustee. The trustee holds this title for the benefit of the lender, who is called the *beneficiary*.

If the borrower does not pay, the lender directs the *trustee* to start a foreclosure. This *non-judicial foreclosure* involves the process of selling the property to a third-party bidder or, in the absence of a sufficient third-party bid, the *beneficiary* acquires title to the property. The foreclosure sale, in most cases, satisfies the debt.

If you need to direct the trustee to start a non-judicial foreclosure, you may or may not be able to recover the entire loan balance. For example, if a third party bids at a non-judicial foreclosure sale an amount equal to or greater than the amount which you are owed (including attorneys fees, costs, and expenses of the foreclosure) you would be fully paid.

Land Contract

A *land contact* comes about in a situation similar to the purchase money mortgage. Instead of giving a deed and taking back a promissory note secured by a mortgage, the seller enters into a land contract with the buyer in which the buyer promises to pay for the land. Ordinarily the buyer promises to pay in installments over a period of time. In the same contract, the seller promises to deed the property to the buyer when the purchase price is fully paid.

Notes:

_____

_____

_____

_____

_____

_____

_____

_____

_____

_____

_____

_____

Notes:

Creation of a Seller Carry-back Note

The following discussion also applies to first and second position liens with minor modifications. This type of transaction usually occurs because there are not enough prospective buyers who can qualify for institutional financing. If there were, there **would** be no need for the seller to take back a note. Even when the buyer can qualify for a loan, the buyer may not have enough for the entire down payment. In this case, the buyer gets a first loan from the institution, and the seller takes back a second note and mortgage.

Because the buyer is able to buy a property that he or she would not otherwise have been able to buy, and because the value of the $90,000 face value note in the secondary mortgage money market is only about $70,000, assuming yields in that market are 15% at the time of this sale, the buyer may be willing to pay more than the current appraised market value of the property. This is true because with a seller carry-back note the buyer doesn't have to pay points, fees and other costs usually associated with an institutional loan.

The seller carry-back note can be structured in an almost limitless variety of ways. The note can be fully amortized with no balloon payment (as in this example), amortized over a number of years, say 30 years, with a balloon payment at say 5 or 10 years. The note could be interest only with a balloon.

It can even have stepped interest payments (for example, 8% in year one, 9% in year two, and 10% in year three through the end of the term), or graduated payments (for example, $500 per month for the first 12 months, $600 per month in year two, $700 in year three, etc.). The value of the note in the secondary mortgage money market depends on all of these parameters and more.

Here Is A Typical Example:

A free and clear property (with no existing loans) was sold for $100,000. BUYER gave SELLER a $10,000 cash down payment and SELLER carried back a purchase money Note and Mortgage for $90,000. SELLER was unsuccessful trying to sell it for $90,000 cash (the appraised value). Potential buyers would have had to pay all cash or qualify for a loan.

SELLER offered to sell the property for $100,000 with 10% cash down payment to attract more buyers.

This sale is equivalent to selling the property for $80,000 cash because the SELLER would get about $70,000 for the note if he sold it immediately to a note investor, assuming the market yield for these types of notes was 15% in the secondary mortgage money market.

Notes:

_____

_____

_____

_____

_____

_____

_____

_____

_____

_____

_____

_____

How should an investor structure a note?

Structuring a note, or "writing paper" as it is often called in the industry, allows the investor tremendous flexibility in not only HOW to make a profit, but WHEN. For example, examine the three notes below. They are all fully amortizing. The interest rate is the rate stated in the example. Each has equal monthly installment payments.

Which One Has The Greatest Value?

Note #1: 60 months, 10% interest, $2,124.70 per month

Note #2: 120 months, 8% interest, $1,213.28 per month

Note #3: 180 months, 6% interest, $ 843.86 per month

Believe it or not, all three notes have the same present value of $100,000. Do they have the same value to the note investor? You must ask the question, are you going to own the note as a personal investment, or are you going to broker the note to another investor?

If you are going to broker the paper, that is sell it to another investor for profit, then the return on the investment is the primary issue. The investor will be buying the note, and therefore wants his capital returned quickly. More sooner than later is better. The investor is concerned with achieving the highest rate of return possible, and will seek the highest discount possible. If you structure the note with the largest payments possible, over the shortest period possible, the discount will be less. This is the reason note investors don't like balloon payments or interest only loans. They have to wait a longer period of time to have their investment returned to them. Again, the old principles of time value of money apply.

If you are creating the note for your own personal investment, then the investment objective is just the opposite. You would seek to have the income stream paid over the longest period possible. In this case, most of the payments on the front end of the note are applied to interest rather than principal. You want small payments over a longer period of time.

Let us reexamine the notes in our example above. If the note buyer requires a 15% yield on all three notes, what are they worth? The financial calculator provides the answer.

Note #1 $89,311.09

Note #2: $75,202.30

Note #3: $60,293.27

The reason for the difference is that Note #1 returns the investor's money the fastest. If you were going to broker the $100,000 note, you would structure it more like Note #1 than Note #3. Which note will pay the most money over the life of the note?

Note #1 60 months x $2,124.70 = $127,482.00

Note #2: 120 months x $1,213.28 = $145,593.60

Note #3: 180 months x $843.86 = $151,894.80

Note #1 provides an income stream for 5 years. While Note #3 provides an income stream for 15 years. It is not the face amount of the note or the stated interest rate or the term of the note that determines its value, but other factors such as who will own the note, and for what purpose is the note being created. If I am "writing paper" to sell, I would write Note #1. It is easier to sell, and the discount would be less. However, if I am "writing paper" for my own personal investment, I would write Note #3.

Ten necessary elements of a promissory note

(1) **Origination date:** The date the note was created. It is a reference date and should conform to the same reference date on the security instrument. The security instrument will reference a "note or notes of even date."

(2) **Date interest begins (most often it is different from the origination date):** When a note calls for interest payments, interest usually begins accruing from the closing date of the sale. It is most often payable in arrears.

(3) **Date of the first payment:** The day of the month (or period) when each payment is due. The payer must pay on or before this date. It is also the reference point (beginning of the grace period) to determine when late charges apply. Payments may be monthly, quarterly, semi-annual, annual, or whatever specific dates the parties agree on.

(4) **Date the balloon payment, if any, is due:** This usually is the date that the final payment of principal and interest is due and payable.

(5) **Principal amount of the note (sometimes referred to as the face amount, principal, or original amount of the note):** This is the amount owed and the amount to be paid by the payer.

(6) **Name of the payer(s) (who pays):** The borrower.

(7) **Name of the payee(s) (who received the payment):** In this book the property seller on a seller carry-back note.

(8) **Location where payments are to be sent:** The payer must know where to make his regular payment. If the payee moves, he should notify the payer where to send the payment.

(9) **Interest rate (typically written as an annual rate even though the payment is paid monthly):** A vital element in the note. What the seller receives as a rate of return must be clearly spelled out.

(10) **Amount of the payment to be made in each period:** This figure should be specific to avoid any misunderstanding.

Notes:

What is discounted paper?

In this area of investment, when I use the term "PAPER" I am referring to the purchasing of promissory notes secured by real estate. In the State of Georgia, these notes are secured by what is known as a Security Deed or a Deed to Secure Debt. In the states of Florida and Alabama and other states they are called Mortgages. In a number of states they are called Trust Deeds. For the purposes of this course, they can all be treated the same. There are many types of paper such as accounts receivable, automobile paper, mobile home paper, annuities, lottery winnings, etc.

Becoming a millionaire is simple

Investing as little as $200 per month can create a net cash return of over a million dollars by retirement. All one really needs is to understand the principles of "compounding" and "discounting." The most valuable lesson one can ever learn in the financial world is the Time Value of Money. Baron Von Rothschild described compound interest as "the eighth wonder of the world."

A Penny a Day

Suppose you were offered a salary of. $25,000 per month or a salary of a penny a day, which doubles every day for 30 days (meaning on the second day you would he paid $.02, and on the third day you would be paid $.04 and so forth). Which would you take? What if you were offered a salary of $50,000 per month, or a lump sum payment of $1,000,000? If you selected a penny a day, which doubled everyday for 30 days, you would receive $10,737,418.23. What happens if you withdrew some money on say the fifteenth day? We will find out what this would do to your financial picture.

Compound interest

Peter Minuet is said to have purchased the island of Manhattan in the year 1626 for about $24 worth of beads. If instead of buying Manhattan had he put the $24 into a hank account paying 6% compound interest per year and left the money there continuously, today he would have a bank account of approximately $65 billion, ignoring income taxes. I guess we have to judge for ourselves whether Peter made a wise purchase.

However, to carry the illustration a step further, notice how slowly Peter Minuet's account would have grown in the first 300 years. He had not accumulated that critical mass. By 1925 he wouldn't even have been a billionaire! He really would have grown fabulously wealthy only in the past 60 years. In 1998 alone he would have made $3,522,998,645. Remember that the rate of growth of his wealth was constant throughout the period, 6% per year. It is the gain each year that accelerates under compound interest.

Year	Ending Balance	Gain from Previous Year
1626	$24	$1
1675	$417	$24
1725	$7,682	$435
1775	$141309	$8,010
1825	$2,606,624	$147,545
1875	$48,014,421	$2,717,797
1925	$884,433,035	$50,062,247
1940	$2,119,595,236	$119,977,089
1975	$16,291,392,953	$922,154,318
1992	$43,869,019,586	$2,483,152,052
1993	$46,501,160,761	$2,632,141,175
1994	$49,291,230,407	$2,790,069,646
1995	$52,248,704,231	$2,957,473,824
1996	$55,383,626,485	$3,134,922,254
1997	$58,706.644.075	$3,323,017,589
1998	$62,229,042,719	$3,522,398,645
1999	$65,962,785,282	$3,733.742,563
2000	$69,920,552,399	$3,957,767.117

To verify the above figures you will need to adjust your financial calculator to compute annual compounding rather than the default monthly compounding. Consult your financial calculator manual

How to discount paper

There arc two elements of a note payment. There is the principal portion, and there is the interest portion. For example, a payment of $728.39 may break down into $364.92 principal and $363.47 interest. If the same note is bought at a discount, the payment breaks down into principal, interest, and discount or what is known as yield. When you calculate your rate of return you calculate your discount (yield) in the same place on the financial calculator as you previously calculated the interest.

Discounting means calculating the "Present Value" of a single series of payments. To accomplish this task, the first step is to identify the "Present Value" of a single series of payments. There are three types of cash flows a note may have. They are:

(1) Single Payment

(2) Series of Payments

(3) Series of Payments Beginning at a Future Date,

In order to calculate the present value of a series of payments, the payments must be in the same amount for each payment, and the payments must have an equal time period between each payment.

There are two ways to determine the price of a note to be bought and the yield of that note:

(1) The first, easiest, and quickest way is to use a financial calculator.

(2) The second method of discounting cash flows involves the use of yield tables. Very few people use the yield tables anymore.

Regardless of the financial calculator used, the process is the same, even though different calculators use different steps. The five keys we will be using on the financial calculator are labeled:

N

I/Y

PV

PMT

FV

Generally, only four of the keys (variables) are used at any one time. When three of these variables are known, the calculator will solve for the unknown variable.

Each of the keys on the calculator stands for one of the variables on the note:

N = Number of payments or any time period such as number of months or years

I/Y = Interest Rate or Yield

PV = Present Value

PMT = Payment

FV = Future Value (What is the value at some time in the future).

Usually, when FV is used, PMT is not used, and when PMT is used, FV is not used.

In most of the examples that follow herein, the payments have been rounded. All calculators' use different rounding systems, so if your answer is very close, don't worry,

Negative Numbers

On most of the calculators, when you see a negative number after a cash flow this means that you are paying out a cash flow. Money that you receive in is expressed as a positive number. To illustrate, if you have the following loan on a parcel of real estate, the payment going out is expressed as a negative number, and the principal balance is expressed as a positive number.

360 = N (number of payments)

6 = I/Y (interest rate on loan)

$100,000 = PV (principal balance of loan)

-599.55 = PMT (monthly principal and interest payment on loan)

FV = 0

The $100,000 is a positive figure because it is money coming IN to the borrower. (Loan proceeds). The -$599.55 is the money going OUT. (Monthly loan payment). Any balloon payments to be made in the future would be expressed as a negative (-) because the borrower is paying it OUT sometime in the future.

A lender such as a bank or a mortgage company looks at this just the opposite. The $100,000 would be expressed as a negative since it is money going out. The monthly payment of $599.55 to the lender is expressed as a positive since the lender is receiving it.

In calculating the yield on paper, be aware of the fact that the interest rate stated on the note affects the value or price of the note. The higher the interest rate (yield), the lower the value over a period of time. For example, let's look at a monthly payment of $500 per month for a period of 360 months. Look how much that payment is worth at different interest rates:

N	I/Y	PV	PMT	FV
360	6	-83,395.81	500	N/A
360	8	-68,141.75	500	N/A
360	12	-48 609.17	500	N/A
360	24	-24.979.96	500	N/A

When you have mastered this basic concept of discounting, the whole field of discounted mortgages, notes, interest rates, and yields will shine it's bright light of endless possibilities in investing for cash flow.

Notes:

_____

_____

_____

_____

_____

_____

_____

_____

_____

_____

_____

_____

_____

Amortization explained

Remember the two parts of a mortgage payment:

(1) The principal payment

(2) The interest payment

The lower the interest rate on the note, then more of the payment goes towards paying the principal. Look at the amortization schedule on your home mortgage. During the early payments of the loan, most of the payment is applied to the interest while only a small portion is applied to the principal. With each successive payment, a little more goes towards payment of principal, and that portion applied to the interest payment declines. As the payments progress, the loan balance of principal begins to decrease more rapidly. There are several methods of how you can more rapidly pay off a mortgage by utilizing discount mortgage techniques.

Discounting made simple

Learning how to discount a note is one of the most valuable skills any real estate investor can acquire. It is surprising how many real estate brokers, bankers, mortgage brokers, and investors there are that don't have the slightest clue.

There are three easy steps in discounting a note. Only attempt to do this with a financial calculator. Using banking tables or trying to memorize the financial formulas should be left to those in the academic world or those who DON'T want to make money. All you need to know is what number needs to be entered under what key. So here we go. As the famous football Coach Vince Lombardi would say on the first day of training camp, "Gentlemen, this is a football."

Notes:

Some calculator basics

(1) The calculator is the workhorse. It does all the calculations. Don't be worried about financial formulas, higher math, or any computer skills. You just have to know what number to put under what button. If this liberal arts major can do it, so can you.

(2) All time periods, rates, and payments must be consistent. For example, if the interest rate is entered on a monthly basis, then the payment must be entered on a monthly basis. For example, if you have a 30-year mortgage, it must he expressed on a monthly basis (360 months).

(3) Be sure to enter zeros under the keys not used in your calculation. Many of the mistakes will come from the fact that most calculators will keep the numbers in the memory register until they are either replaced or cleared. There are five keys on the financial calculator that we will be using: N (number), I/Y (interest or yield), PV (present value), PMT (payment), and FV (future value). Only four keys will be used at any one time. The fifth key MAY need to have a zero entered under it or the calculation will be incorrect. In order for your calculation to be correct, enter the zero first.

(4) Long-term loans require large discounts because the discount has to apply over a longer period of time to equal a certain yield. Short-term loans require a smaller amount of discount.

(5) The DISCOUNT AND YIELD ARE NOT SYNONYMOUS. Many people, including experienced real estate investors, confuse these two terms, Discount is the amount that must be subtracted from a loan balance to equal the purchase price that should he paid to obtain a certain yield. Yield, on the other hand, is the effective rate of return that is produced when less than the face value of the note is paid in a cash purchase.

(6) Different financial calculators will round numbers differently so that the answer may be a few cents different from calculator to calculator. If your answer is close within a few cents, don't worry.

(7) If your calculator has a setting of "BEGIN/END", make sure it is set on "END" for all of your calculations.

Notes:

THE THREE MAGIC STEPS

Step 1: Identify All the Cash Flows

Step 2: Solve For Unknown Factors

Step 3: Discount and Add the Cash Flows

Step One: Identify the cash flows

There are three types of cash flows that might be applicable. Any note you might want to discount might have one, two, or all three cash flows. The three different cash flows are:

(1) **Series of Payments:** A Series of Payments is where the same amount is paid in regular intervals over a certain period of time.

(2) **Lump Sum Payment:** A Lump Sum Payment is where only one payment is received at a certain time in the future.

(3) **Future Series of Payments:** A Future Series is where there is a series of payments that do not begin immediately, but begin at a time certain in the future.

The first question you must ask is: "How much cash flow is there?"

The second question is: "What are the cash flows?"

The third question is: "What type of cash flow is it?" The cash flow is determined by how much you receive, when you receive it, or how many times you receive it.

EXAMPLE A:

In this example, the note has a present balance of $25,000. and pays $149.89 per month for 30 years at 6% interest.

(1) How many cash flows? — There is one cash flow.

(2) What is the cash flow? - $149.89 per month for 30 years (360 months)

(3) What type of cash flow? - Series of Payments. (More than one identical payment of $149.89 per month occurring at regular intervals of once a month for 360 months.)

EXAMPLE B:

In this example, the note has a present balance of $10,000 and has no payments for five years. The interest of 10% adds on each year and in five years there is a balloon of $16,105.10.

(1) How many cash flows? - There is only one cash flow.

(2) What is the cash flow? - One payment of $16,105.10 in five years.

(3) What type of cash flow? - Lump Sum Payment because there is only one payment due at a future date.

EXAMPLE C.

In this example, the note has a present balance of $10,000 and no payments for three years with interest at 10%. In three years the balance will be $13,310.00 after annual compounding. At the end of three years, there will be payments of $143.03 per month for the next 15 years (a total of 18 years).

(1) How many cash flows? - There is only one cash flow

(2) What is the cash flow? - The cash flow is $143.03 per month for 180 months that begins in 3 years

(3) What type of cash flow? - There is a series of payments of $143.03 per month for 180 months that does not begin until a future date. Therefore, this is a Future Series of Payments Cash Flow.

EXAMPLE D

This is a note with a present balance of $25,000 and an interest rate of 6%. There are payments of $149.89 per month for the first five years (60 months) and then the entire remaining balance of $23,263.59 will he due.

How many cash flows? - There are two cash flows:

(1) What are the cash flows? - The first cash flow is $149.89 per month for 60 months. The second cash flow is one payment of $23,263.59 payable in five years.

(2) What type of cash flows?

    a. Series of Payments

    b. Lump Sum Payment

Step Two: Solving for unknown factors

Dividing a cash flow

You will begin to learn how to divide a cash flow into as many parts as necessary to create a purchase that meets the needs of the note seller.

To prove you can divide a cash flow into many parts and add their Present Values, consider the following balloon note. We will see what we can pay for the whole note, then just the Payments, and then just the Balloon Payment. We want a 19% yield in each case.

Seller offers you the following note;

Box #1: Clear your calculator. Calculate the Pmt

N	I/Y	PV	Pmt	FV
This is the number of payments.	This is the face interest rate,	This is the present value of the note when it was created.	Calculate the monthly payment	This is the balloon amount on this interest only note.
60	10%	-40,000		40,000
This is the original note.				

You offer to buy the note to yield you 19%.

Box #2: Calculate the PV

N	I/Y	PV	Pmt	FV
This is the number of payments.	This is your required yield to buy this cash flow.	Calculate the price you will pay for the note.	This is the monthly payment from Box #1	This is the balloon amount on this interest only note.
60	19%		333.33	40,000
PV is the price you will pay for the whole note.				

Seller says, "No way, that's too much of a discount! And I need the monthly income for my car Payments." You say, "Okay, I will buy just the Balloon Payment and you can keep the monthly Payments."

Box #3: Calculate the PV

N	I/Y	PV	Pmt	FV
This is the number of the months you must wait for the balloon payments.	This is your required yield to buy this cash flow.	*Calculate the price you will pay for the balloon payment (FV) in N months.*	This is $0 because all the payments will go to the note seller.	This is the amount you will receive in N months.
60	19		0	40,000
Pmt is $0 because those Payments will go to seller.				

In 60 months, you will get the Balloon Payment of $40,000 for an initial investment of $15,585.20. Seller adds up the 60 payments of $333.33 and finds she will get $19,999.80 in Payments plus $15,585.20 from you today. This total of $35,585 seems like a better deal than selling the whole note. However, she is still skeptical. You say, "Look, I can buy just the 60 Payments and you can have the $40,000 Balloon Payments in 60 months. Here's how that looks:

Box #4: Calculate the PV

N	I/Y	PV	Pmt	FV
This is the number of payments you are buying.	This is your required yield to buy this cash flow.	Calculate the price you will pay for the payment (Pmt) in N months.	You are buying this payment stream.	This is so because the balloon payment will now go to the note seller
60	19		333.33	0
FV is $0 because the Balloon Payment will go to Seller in 60 months.				

Now, Seller thinks she has figured on the best deal. She gets $12,849.77 now from you (PV in Box #4) and the $40,000 balloon in 60 months. She adds these figures together and gets $52,849.77 for her $40,000 note.

She, like most people, does not understand that $40,000 to be received in 60 months is worth less than $40,000 today. She erroneously adds all the Payments together and gets another figure that does not mean anything to the sophisticated calculator user. You should never add money now and money to be received in the future, but sellers will always do that every time. Therefore, we accommodate them.

However, the lesson for the note broker is this: The Present Value of just the Balloon Payment at 19% in Box #3 is $15,585.20. The Present Value of just the Payment Stream in Box #4 is $12,849.77. If we add the Present Value of the Payment stream and the Present Valve of the Future Value or Balloon Payment, we get a total of $28,434.97. This is what we calculated in Box #2. This is the amount we can pay for the whole note.

In short, the present value (PV) of just the payments (Pmt), plus the present value (PV) of just the balloon (FY) equals the present value (PV) of the entire note.

What You Have Learned: The only time you can legitimately add cash flows together is when they have all been reduced to their Present Value.

Box #1:	Pmt = $333.33
Box #2:	PV = $28,435.10
Box #3:	PV = $15,585.20
Box #4:	PV = $12,849.77

Notes:

_____

_____

_____

_____

_____

_____

_____

Calculating the balance due on a note

There are at least three ways to calculate the balance due on a note after several payments have been made. This section will explore the PV method and the FV method. If you have a "balance due" key on your financial calculator, it is worth the effort to learn to use it. You will seldom see a new note, and you need to he able to calculate the Present Value on any note.

Balance due: Present Value (PV) method

You will learn one way to find the amount due on a note after several payments have been made.

Unfortunately, we seldom see a cash flow where the *balance due* on the note is the same as the face value of the note. Usually, several payments have been made to the note seller before she decides to sell.

You are offered the following note:

Box #1: Clear your calculator. Calculate the Pmt

N	I/Y	PV	Pmt	FV
The months to amortize or payoff the PV in full.	Face interest rate on the note.	The amount of money borrower	Calculate the payment on this note.	There is no balloon payment on this note.
360	10	-100,000		0
This is the original note.				

The seller informs you that she has been receiving payments on this note for five years and she would like to sell you the note. You agree to buy it to yield you 15% because you know you can broker it to a corporate note buyer for a lower yield, and consequently a higher price, and a larger commission. First, you need to calculate the balance still due to Seller. Since she has received 5 years worth of Payments, the *balance due* is less than $100,000.

Using the PV *method*, you must put into N the number of Payments remaining to be paid and calculate the Present Value.

Box #2: Calculate the PV

N	I/Y	PV	Pmt	FV
This is the number of payments remaining to be paid.	Face interest rate on the note	Calculate the balance due on this note.	This is the monthly payment from Box #1 above.	There is no balloon payment on this note.
300	10		877.57	0
60 monthly payments have gone to Seller.				

You are only able to buy the 300 remaining Payments, so the Present Value (PV) is the *balance due* on this note. If you want to buy it to yield you 15%, you must use the figures in Box #2.

Box #3: Calculate the PV

N	I/Y	PV	Pmt	FV
This is the number of payments remaining to be paid	Your required yield to buy this cash flow.	Calculate the amount you will pay for this note to achieve your (I/Y) yield.	This is the monthly payment from Box #1 above.	There is no balloon payment on this note.
300	15		877.57	0
The PV is what the note is worth today at a 15% yield.				

What You Have Learned: Put N into the number of Payments *remaining* and recalculate the Present Value (PV) to get the *balance due* on a note.

Box #1:	Pmt = $877.57
Box #2:	PV = - $96,574.32
Box #3:	PV = - $68,515.82

Balance due: The FV Method

You will learn another way to calculate the balance due on a note after several payments have been made.

The seller offers you the following note from the previous chapter: Clear your calculator. Calculate the N

N	I/Y	PV	Pmt	FV
Calculate the number of payments originally for this note.	This is the face interest rate on the note.	This is the amount of money borrowed.	This is the monthly payment required fully to amortize the note in N months.	There is no balloon payment on this note.
	10	-100,000	877.57	0
This is the original note				

She tells you she has received 60 Payments. What is the *balance due* on the note using the FV method? Here we put the Payments made (not Payments remaining) into N and calculate the Future Value (FV).

Box #2: Calculate the FV

N	I/Y	PV	Pmt	FV
This is the number of payments made on the note.	This is the face interest rate on the note.	This is the amount of money borrowed.	This is the monthly Payment required fully to amortize the note in N months.	Calculate the Balance due on this slate after N payments have been made.
60	10	-100,000	877.57	
This is the original note.				

FV is the *Balance due* and should be the same as in the previous chapter. However, it's off by a few cents! The reason is: I tricked you!

Here's what happened. In the previous chapter, you calculated the Payment (pmt) to be $877.57 but your calculator showed you only the first two digits in the cents column as .57. Your calculator carried the answer out to as many as 13 decimal places. Therefore, the *real* Payment on this note in the previous chapter is $877.57 if you calculated the Pmt. However, in this chapter, I told you to enter only 877.57 in the Pmt column and it is a slightly wrong answer! Therefore, since we don't usually see all the digits to the right of the decimal point, we entered a truncated payment (PMT). That is why your answers may be slightly different than those throughout this book

This is why your answers may not always agree with ours. Any difference under about $2 is of no consequence. It is a function of how you entered the numbers.

You can get the same answer in FV that you did in the previous chapter if you put 360 into N and recalculate the Pmt. Pmt then will have all the digits and your FV calculation in Box #2 above will be identical to the PV in the previous chapter.

To see all the digits, consult your calculator manual to learn how to change the screen to display all the digits to the right of the decimal point.

What You Have Learned: Put into N the payments made and keep all the parameters the same and calculate the Future Value (FV) to get the *balance due* on the note. Remember that your calculator carried out its calculations to more decimal places than are visible on your screen.

Box #1: N = 360

Box #2: FV = $96,574.44

Step Three: Discounting

You will learn how to discount a cash flow to give you your desired yield.

If you were to buy a $20,000 note, 15-year term, 12% interest, what would you buy the note for? Would you pay $20,000? Or would you pay less? If your investment strategy was to have each invested dollar earn 20%, you couldn't buy that note for a "full price" of $20,000 since you would only be earning 12% interest.

To get your 20% return or yield, you would have to pay less than the $20,000. This is the concept of discounting cash flows. Though you pay less for the note, the monthly Payments won't change. In this case, they'll still be $240.03 each month. So, the question really is: If you're receiving Payments of $240.03 (pmt) for 15 years (N), how much must you pay to get a 20% (IN) yield?

First calculate the parameters of the original note:

Box #1: Clear your calculator Calculate the Pmt

N	I/Y	PV	Pmt	FV
This is the number of payments in the note. 15 years = 180 months.	This is the face interest rate on the note.	This is the amount of money borrowed.	Calculate the monthly payment required to fully amortize the note in N months.	There is no balloon payment on this note.
180	12	-20.000		
This is the original note				

We want to calculate the Present Value of this note at our required yield. We put yield in the I/Y register and then calculate the PV.

Box #2: Calculate the PV

N	I/Y	PV	Pmt	FV
Calculate the number of payments originally for this note.	The yield you want to make on your purchase of this cash flow	Calculate the amount of money needed to buy this note to achieve the I/Y yield.	This is the monthly Payment required fully to amortize the note in N months, from Box #1	There is no balloon payment on this note.
180	20		240.03	0
The PV is the amount you will pay for this cash flow to get a 20°/o yield.				

Answer: PV $13,667.03. By paying $13,667 for this stream of Payments, you will have a yield of 20% per year. You would present this offer to the seller of this note.

If any of this is unclear to you, you will have trouble with the rest of this course.

What You Have Learned: Discounting means raising your "yield" in the I/Y column and calculating the PV or Present Value to find the price you will pay for the note.

Box #1: Pmt = $240.03

Box #2: PV = -$13,667.03

Sale of a seller carry-back note

A secured real estate note can he sold at any time from the day it was created until the day of the last payment. What is actually being sold is the stream of monthly payments. A note holder can sell all the payments (full sale) or part of the payments (partial sale).

There are so many options available to the note holder for full and partial sales; they are too numerous to mention. If the note holder is working with a knowledgeable note buyer, the note buyer can structure options designed specifically for the cash needs of the note holder.

It is important to know that all of these sales are equivalent. In other words, a note buyer would be equally happy with any of these purchases from a note holder.

Example of a $90,000 Note On Which You Are Receiving Payments:

Sales Price of Property = $95,000

Loan To Value = S84,257/$95,000 = 89%

Buyer's Equity $10,742.67

- $90,000 Face Value Note
- 10% Interest Rate
- 15-Year Term (180 Payments)
- $967.14 Monthly Payments
- 24 payments have been made. The current Balance owed is $84,257.19

First Mortgage $84,257.19   Owed Now

Some of the options available to the note holder

1. **DO NOTHING.** Continue receiving the remaining *156* monthly payments of $967.14.

2. **FULL SALE.** Sell the entire note now.

   NOTE HOLDER GETS: $66,229.74   **CASH NOW** (15 % yield)

3. **PARTIAL SALE-FRONT END PAYMENTS.** Sell the next 5 years of payments (60 payments). Then receive the last 96 payments.

   NOTE HOLDER GETS: $ 40,653.53   **CASH NOW** (15% yield)
                       $ 63,736.27   <u>Loan Balance in 5 years (10% of face amt)</u>
                       $104,389.80   **Total Cash to Note Holder**

4. **FULL SALE-SPLIT FUNDING.** Sell one half of the note (the next 78 payments) now and the other half of the note (the remaining 78 payments) after the first 78 payments are paid.

   NOTE HOLDERS GETS: $48,010.70   **CASH NOW** (78 pmts at 15% yield.)
                       $48,010.70   <u>Cash in 78 months</u>
                       $96,021.40   **Total Cash in Note Holder**

5. **PARTIAL SALE-ONE HALF OF EACH MONTHLY PAYMENT.** Sell one half of each monthly payment and continue to receive the other half.

   NOTE HOLDER GETS: $33,114.72   **CASH NOW**
                         $ 483.57   Per Month for 156 Months

Many other options are available. Options can be designed specifically for the cash needs of the Note Holder.

Full Sale

When the entire note is sold, it is always sold at a "discount" off the current principal balance of the note, The reason for this is that the face interest rate of the note is seldom as high as the market yield required in the secondary mortgage money market. In the foregoing example, the discount is $18,027.90 ($84,257.33 minus $66,229.43) assuming the secondary mortgage money market yield is 15%. The discount could be more or less depending on the current yield requirements in the secondary mortgage money market.

Partial Sale-Front End Payments

Partial sales are very attractive from the point of view of a note holder because the note holder does not have to take a big discount. The main reason for the discount being so large ($18,027.90 in the example) is that the payments due in the distant future are worth much less in today's dollars than the payments that are due soon.

In a full sale, the note holder is selling all the payments, and is not receiving much money from the payments at the end of the 15-year term—thus the large discount. In a partial sale where the front-end or near term payments are sold, most of the payment is interest. This means that the note holder gets a sizable amount of cash now ($40,653.53 in the example) and when the note holder gets the note back after 60 payments, the balance of the note is still fairly high ($63,736.27 in the example). The note holder then gets the remaining 96 payments of $967.14.

A partial sale of the front-end payments is like having your cake and eating it, too. You get a sizable chunk of cash now, and when you get the note back, it has a high remaining principal balance and many payments left to collect.

In the example, the cash the note holder receives now plus the remaining loan balance the note holder receives in 5 years is more than $20,000 higher than the current principal balance of the note. In many cases, note holders prefer this type of an arrangement rather than selling the entire note for a large discount off the current principal balance.

Full Sale-Split Funding

In the split-funded sale, the note holder is selling all of the payments but is only selling part of the payments now and part of the payments in the future. This type of sale is really a hybrid between a full sale and a partial sale.

In the example, one half of the note (the next 78 payments) is sold now and the other half of the note (the last 78 payments) is sold after the first 78 payments are paid. $48,010.70 is paid in cash now and an equal amount in 6 1/2 years.

This is only one variation of a split-funded sale. The note could be split into three, four or more equal or unequal parts.

Partial Sale-One Half Of Each Monthly Payment

In this type of a sale, the note holder sells one half of each monthly payment and continues to receive the other half. This is a particularly attractive way to sell a note if you need some cash now but also want to keep part of the monthly cash now. The example shows that one half of each of the 156 remaining payments can be sold for $33,114.72 and $483.57 keeps coming in every month. Again, this is only one variation of this type of sale. Many different variations are available to suit your needs as a note holder.

Tax Reporting For Note Holders

When real property is sold, and a purchase money note and mortgage are carried back by the seller as part or the entire purchase price of the property, the gain on the sale is reported on the seller's tax return as an installment sale.

The amount of interest received each year by the seller or note holder must be reported on Schedule B of Form 1040. This is a very simple process if the note holder has an amortization schedule for the loan, which summarizes the interest portion of each payment received.

A portion of the principal received each year must also be reported on Schedule D of Form 1040 (and supporting Form 6251 for Installment Sales). This is not as simple as the tax reporting for interest.

The total amount of the gain on the sale is called the *realized gain*. Realized gain is the net sales price less the cost. The amount of the realized gain that is reported each year on the note holder's tax return is called *recognized gain.*

This is a simplified explanation and competent tax advice should he sought when determining tax liability due when buying and selling notes.

Notes:

Checklist to use before you agree to carry-back a note or before you buy an existing note.

1. **Get a credit report on buyers of the property**

   Sellers should get the property buyers' social security number and the property buyers' written permission to run a credit check. This will assure the sellers that buyers are people with a history of paying their bills on time.

   (A sample Credit Report Authorization letter is in the Appendix.)

2. **Try to get a current financial statement on the buyers**

   This becomes important in states where the buyer has personal liability when signing a carry-back note secured by real estate.

3. **If there is any doubt about the value of a substitute property, then get an independent appraisal from a professional appraiser, one <u>you select</u> who is licensed and not in the business of marketing real estate.**

   This should be available for a few hundred dollars on a small property. On an apartment or office building, the cost could easily be several thousand dollars or more.

4. **Prior to closing, get a loan status report for any senior loan to insure that it is current**.

   Watch out for negative amortization. If a senior lien has an adjustable interest rate or payment amount, the loan may allow negative amortization (when the interest payment is greater than the total payment, interest not covered by the total payment and is added to the loan balance). Negative amortization can quickly erode the **protective equity** of a junior lien holder. Even without negative amortization, increases in the interest rate on an Adjustable Rate Mortgage (ARM) will increase the monthly payment, which could eventually force the payer into default. Such an ARM note increases the risk to anyone holding a junior note behind a first mortgage with an adjustable interest rate.

5. **Look for a due-on-sale provision in the first loan documents**.

If the loan has such a clause and you are forced to foreclose, the first loan holder can call his loan due and payable in full. The reason is that after foreclosure, the former owner/borrower has alienated (gone out of) title. To prevent this from happening, try to get the first loan holder to sign a Non-Acceleration Letter. That is your best protection. It protects you in acquiring the property through foreclosure if you keep their loan current. If you resell, then they still have the right to accelerate their loan unless they approve the new buyer.

6. **Get a Preliminary Title Report or a Commitment To Insure from an established, reputable title insurance company on any property that will be used to secure the newly created note.**

This will protect you against a flawed title, liens or other encumbrances that could cause future problems.

7. **If your state laws provide for it, record a Request for Notice of Default**.

When recorded, this Request for Notice requires a senior lien holder to notify junior holders in the event the senior holder commences a foreclosure action.

8. **Notice to Senior Lender.**

In states which have no provision for such default notices, a good idea for you as a junior lien holder is to notify the senior lien holder in writing that you hold a junior lien and you would like to be notified in the event he does not receive his payment within thirty days of its due date. The senior note holder will usually respond, as he wants to know that his loan will be paid by you if his borrower does not pay.

9. **Be sure that the Mortgagor carries fire Insurance at least equal to the replacement cost of the improvements and that you are named as a mortgagee/loss payee.**

If the improvements burn down, you'll be protected.

10. **Check once a year with the county tax collector to make sure the Mortgagor has paid his property taxes.**

Institutional lenders frequently employ a tax service to do this. Nonpayment of either fire insurance and/or property taxes constitutes a default on most loans and may give you the right to foreclose. Foreclosure procedures are important.

11. Understand the foreclosure laws in your state.

12. If the entity signing the note is a partnership or a corporation, seek legal advice. additional safeguards may he needed.

13. *When buying a note, get an Offset Statement, Statement of Balance Due, or Estoppel Letter. They all mean about the same.*

This should be signed by the current mortgagor confirming that the balance due and other terms of the note concur with what the note seller has told you and confirmed in writing on a Beneficiary Statement. Getting a written statement prevents future problems.

14. Personal guarantees (when a note is being sold, with recourse)

Note buyers may ask note sellers to personally guarantee the note being purchased. This means that if the payer does not pay and the note buyer forecloses and does not receive payment in full, then the note seller will make up the difference.

Notes:

_____

_____

_____

_____

_____

Notes:

What is your note worth?

Another way of asking this question is, "How much of a discount must I take if I sell my note?" All notes are purchased at less than the remaining balance of the note if the whole note is purchased. This difference between the remaining balance and the purchase price of the note is the "discount."

There is no standard discount because there are no standard notes or standard properties. Each note is different and each note must be individually researched in order to determine its highest value.

If you do not need all the cash from your note immediately, it is possible to receive 100% or more of the remaining balance of your note by selling only a part of the payments on the note now.

The best way to find out how much your note is worth is to get a quotation from a professional note buyer. Be wary of some people who may approach you offering to buy your note for cash. Many of these buyers will attempt to give you a low-ball offer, whereas a professional note buyer will be more competitive with current secondary mortgage money market rates.

Also, many amateur note buyers don't know how to structure partial offers tailored to your needs as a note holder and many don't know how to close the transaction properly so both the note holder and the note buyer are protected.

Notes:

Solving the cash problem

You will learn how to give the note seller a certain amount of cash by buying a specific number of payments.

If a seller calls you with a note to sell and with a need for a specific amount of cash, you should be able to provide it. In fact, you will see this can be the most lucrative situation since the number of payments you buy can effectively solve the seller's problem and still leave a good commission for yourself.

Providing your seller with a requested amount of cash means you are a good negotiator and listener and have learned exactly what the seller will do with the money. The business of purchasing notes is a people business and the profits go to the note broker who can effectively use both people skills and calculator skills.

A seller calls you with a $60,000, 10% interest rate, 10 year note she wants to sell. Through skillful listening, you learn she needs just $15,000 to pay for her two children's dental work. How much of the note (N) will you buy if you require a 24% yield (I/Y)? How much of the note you buy depends on how many payments you buy.

The original note looks like this:

Box #1: Clear your calculator. Calculate the Pmt

N	I/Y	PV	Pmt	FV
Original number of payments.	Face interest Rate on the note,	The amount of money the payer owes the seller.	Calculate the payment on the note.	There is no balloon payment.
120	10	-60,000		0
This is the note she wishes to sell.				

Now- calculate how many payments you can buy.

Fill in the known parameters of the note and solve for the unknown. You know you want a 24% yield, so put that into I/Y. You know she wants $15,000, so put that into PV. Make sure to enter it as a negative number. You know the Payment is $792.90, so put that into Pmt. You know there is no Balloon Payment, so enter 0 in FV. The only parameter left to solve is the number of Payments you will buy.

Box #2: Calculate the N

N	I/Y	PV	Pmt	FV
Calculate N	Your yield.	Money she needs.	Payments.	No Balloon
24		-15,000.00	792.90	0
Solve for the number of payments you will buy to earn 24%.				

Answer: 24.01 Payments. Should you round down to 24 Payments, or would it be better to round up to buy 25 or 27 or 29 Payments? There is not one seller in a hundred that would or could tell the difference. Let your conscience be your guide.

Here's how it looks on your calculator:

What is your yield if you round up to buying 27 Payments?

Box #3: Calculate the I/Y

N	I/Y	PV	Pmt	FV
This is the number of payments you might buy.	Calculate your yield by buying N payments	This is the amount of money Seller needs	The payment calculated in Box #1.	There is no balloon payment
27		-15,000	792.90	0
You are solving for our new yield				

You could buy 28 or 29 Payments; but don't let greed keep you from closing the deal!

See if you can calculate the balance clue on the note when Seller gets the note back. ($51.172.25)

What have you learned? If you know the amount of money the note seller needs, you can calculate the number of Payments you can buy.

Box #1: Pmt = $792.90

Box #2: N = 24.01 Payments. Note: *if you* are using an HP-12C financial calculator, it will only calculate whole numbers for N. Simply leave it and recalculate FV to find the small balloon payment.

Box #3:   I/Y= 32.82%

Five offers on one note

You will learn there are many ways to purchase a cash flow. Your success depends on your ability to create an offer that exactly meets the note seller's needs.

Here are additional ways to provide a note seller with a specific amount of cash. Success as a note broker requires an understanding of cash flows, which we hope you are learning in this course. It also requires the ability to help a note seller by buying his note in a creative way that solves his problem.

A man calls you with a note he wishes to sell. The terms of the note are as follows:

Box #1: Clear your calculator. Calculate the Pmt

N	I/Y	PV	Pmt	FV
Payments remaining on the note.	The face interest the on Rate note .	The amount of money borrowed.	*Calculate the payment on the note.*	The balloon payment due in N months.
60	12	-50,000		50,000
This is the note you are buying.				

You talk with him about the note and why he wants to sell it. As you talk and establish some rapport. you find out that the note is not a problem so he is not trying to get rid of it. You find he just had his old '79 Dodge "died" on him and he needs to buy a new car. You ask him how much be needs for this new car. It turns out to be around $15,000. This is where you separate yourself from the crowd. You tell him that not only can he sell just a part of his note; you can offer him several ways to do this.

By being able to make several offers based on his need for $15,000, you are clearly showing your skill, flexibility, and the desire to help him.

So let's look at several offers. You want a yield of 18%. Therefore, throughout your calculations, two parameters will remain the same: I/Y or Interest will be 18% and PV, or the amount you will pay for the note, will be $15,000.

OFFER #1: BUY A FEW PAYMENTS

Put $0 into FV. This let's the Balloon (FV) go to the note seller.

Box #2: Clear your calculator. Calculate the N

N	I/Y	PV	Pmt	FV
Calculate the number payments you can buy	This is your Required yield	The amount of cash the seller needs immediately.	The calculated payment from Box #1.	The balloon payment is $0 because it will go the note seller.
	18	-15.000	500	0
You can buy 40 (N) payments or more (Pmt) to give the seller $15,000 (PV).				

(Change N to 41 to an even number and solve for PV = $15,229.48). You receive the first 41 payments, The seller receives the last 19 Payments of $500 plus the balloon of $50,000. Remember, the payer on the note in Box #1 must pay a balloon (PV) of $50,000. However, you the note buyer, did not buy his balloon (FV = $0 in Box #2 above) so the $50,000 goes to the note seller.

SUMMARY: Seller Gets: $15,229.48 immediately
          Last 19 monthly Payments of $500 (or $9,500)
          Balloon of $50 000 in 60 month
TOTAL CASH TO SELLER: $74,729.48

Note Buyer pays $15,229.48 and gets: Next 41 Payments of $500 for a yield of 18%.

OFFER #2: BUY PART OF THE BALLOON

Put 0 into Payment to let all the Payments go to the note seller.

Box #3: Calculate the FV

N	I/Y	PV	Pmt	FV
Number of payments remaining on the note	Your required yield	The amount of money the note seller needs	The payment is $0 because they will all go to the seller	Calculate the portion of the balloon you will buy. The rest will revert to the note seller
60	18	-15,000	0	
You will only buy part of the balloon. All the payments will go to the note seller.				

You pay $15,000 to the seller and you get $36,648 in 60 months and earn 18% on your $15,000 investment. The seller gets $15,000 today and 60 Payments of $500 and $13,151.70 when the balloon of $50.000 is paid (you get $36,648 of the $50,000 and the remaining $13,351 goes to the seller).

SUMMARY: Seller gets:

$15,000 immediately
60 monthly Payments of $500 (or $30,000)
<u>A Balloon Payment in 60 mouths of $13,351.70</u>

TOTAL CASH TO SELLER: $58.351.70

Note Buyer pays $15,000 and gets: A Balloon Payment in 60 months of $36,648.30 for a yield of 18%.

OFFER #3: HALF OF EACH PAYMENT AND PART OF THE BALLOON.

Divide the $500 payment in half and place $250 into Pmt. The other $250 goes to the note seller each month.

Box #4: Clear your Calculator. Calculate the FV

N	I/Y	PV	Pmt	FV
This is the number of payments you will buy	Your required yield	The amount of money the note seller needs	This is ½ of the $500 payment. The other half will go to the note seller each month	Calculate how much of the balloon you will buy
60	18	-15,000	250	
You are offering to buy 1/2 of <u>each</u> monthly payment and part of the $50,000 balloon payment.				

You pay $15,000 to the seller and you get 60 Payments of $250 *and* $12,594.63 of the $50,000 balloon when it is paid and earn 18% on your $15,000 investment. The seller received $15,000 today and 60 Payments of $250 plus a balloon of $37,405.37.

SUMMARY: Seller gets:

$15,000 immediately
60 monthly Payments of $250 (or $15,000)
<u>A Balloon Payment in 60 months of $37,405.37</u>

TOTAL CASH TO SELLER: $67,405.37

Note Buyer pays $15,000 and gets: 60 monthly Payments of $250
A Balloon Payment of $12,594.63 in 60 months for a yield of 18%.

SUMMARY: Seller gets:
$15,000 immediately
$119.10 for 60 months ($7,145.92)
<u>A Balloon in 60 months of $50,000.</u>

TOTAL CASH TO SELLER: $72,145.92

Note Buyer pays $15,000 and gets: 60 Payments of $380.90 for a yield of 18%.

Of course, you don't want to make all five offers to the seller. Never make more than three offers. It tends to confuse the note seller if there are too many choices. By talking, questioning, and listening carefully you will know which offers will be best for this particular person in this particular situation.

Certainly, there are more than five workable offers on this note, but these will give you a good idea of the possibilities that are available to you when the seller has a fixed amount of cash in mind that he or she wants from a note.

What you have learned: If the seller needs a specific amount of money immediately, you can tailor your offer to give him or her exactly what he needs.

Box #1: Pmt = $500

Box #2: N = 40.15 (On the HP 12C calculator you will get an even 41 Payments. This calculator is not able to calculate a fractional "N" number of Payments).

Box #3: FV = $36,648.30

Box #4: FV = 12,594.63

Box #5: Pmt = $121.07

Box #6: Pmt = $380.90

Note: Due to rounding differences, answers within a few dollars are correct.

OFFER #4: HALF OF THE BALLOON AND PART OF EACH PAYMENT

Divide the Balloon Payment (PV) in half and calculate the portion of each Payment that you can buy.

Box #5: Calculate the Pmt

N	I/Y	PV	Pmt	FV
The number of payments you will buy	Your required yield	The amount of money the note seller needs	Calculate how much of each payment you will purchase	This is half the $50,000 balloon payment. The other $25,000 will go to the note seller
60	18	-15,000	121.07	25,000
You are offering to buy part of the balloon and part of each payment,				

You pay $15,000 to the seller *and* you get 60 Payments of $121.07 *and* $25,000 when the balloon of $50,000 is paid. You earn 18% on your $15,000 investment. The seller receives $15,000 today and 60 Payments of $378.93, plus a balloon of $25,000.

SUMMARY: Seller gets: $15,000 immediately
60 monthly Payments of $378.93 or. $22,735.80
and a
Balloon Payment in 60 months of $25,000.
TOTAL TO SELLER: $62,736.80

Note Buyers Pays $15,000 and gets: 60 monthly Payments of $121.07=.$7264.20, plus
A Balloon Payment in 60 months of $25,000 for a
yield of 18%.

TOTAL: $32,624.20

OFFER #5: PART OF EACH PAYMENT

Put $0 into FV to let the Balloon Payment revert to the Seller. Then calculate how much of each Payment you will buy. The portion of the Payment you *don't buy* will go to the note seller each month.

Box #6: Calculate the Pmt

N	I/Y	PV	Pmt	FV
This is the number of payments you will buy.	Your required yield	The amount of money the note seller needs.	Calculate the amount of each payment you will buy.	The balloon amount of $0 because it will go to the note seller.
60	18	-15,000	380.90	0
You are <u>offering</u> to buy $380.90 of each payment.				

Reverse partials

You will learn how to give a note seller cash plus payments for their note.

This is a way of buying a note such that the first 12 or 24 Payments go to the note seller along with the cash for the remaining Payments. It is an excellent purchase strategy for sellers who need some cash now and need to retain some of the Payments.

The seller has a note to sell but needs the next 12 Payments to pay child support to his ex-wife. The $40,000, 7.75% real estate note is amortized over 15 years. Calculate the parameters on the original note:

Box #1: *Clear your calculator. Calculate the Pmt.*

N	I/Y	PV	Pmt	FV
Number of payments on the original note.	The face interest rate on the note.	The amount of the money loaned.	Calculate the amount of the payment.	There is no balloon payment.
180	7.75	-40,000		0
This is the original note.				

You offer to buy the note using a "reverse partial' in which the next 12 Payments will flow through to seller. You require a 16% yield (me I/Y) and will sell the note at an 11% yield (I/Y). First, neither you nor the note buyer *will* get the first 12 payments, so only 16 Payments (N) will be purchased. First calculate your purchase:

Box #2: *Calculate the PV*

N	I/Y	PV	Pmt	FV
This is the number of payments you will purchase. The first 12 payments will go to the note seller.	Your required yield.	Calculate the value of N payments at I/Y yield	The payment *as calculated* in Box #1	There is no balloon payment
168	16		376.51	0
This is your purchase of 168 Payments at a 16% yield,				

However, the Payments won't start for 12 month so we must *discount the value of the future cash flows back to the present.* Move the PV to FV, make Payments 0, and calculate the new PV

Box #3: Calculate the PV

N	I/Y	PV	Pmt	FV
You must wait N months for the flow in Box #2 to start coming to you.	Your required yield as in Box #2	Discount the value of the cash flow to today.	This is 0 because the payments are imputed in the PV calculated in Box #2.	The value of the cash flow if it were to start immediately.
12	16	21,485.85	0	25,187.24
PV is you what you will pay for 168 Payments that start in 12 months				

Seller agrees to sell you the note for $21,485.85 cash now. He will also receive the next 12 Payments of $376.51 or $4,518.12 for a total of $26.003.97.

If the note buyer will buy the note for an 11% yield, you have to go through all the steps again using a 11% yield. The difference between your "buy" price in Box #3 and the "buy" *price of the note buyer* equals your profit.

You will give the seller $21,485.85 for his note now. He will receive the next 12 payments and the 168 payments that go to the note buyer to begin after 12 months. You will sell the same note to the note buyer for $28,866.03. Your commission is $7,380.18.

What You Have Learned: A reverse partial can resolve a problem for some note sellers by letting them have some of the cash flow plus cash now.

Box #1:   Pmt = $376.51

Box #2:   PV = $25,187.24

Box #3:   PV = $21,485.85

Note: Due to rounding differences, answers within few dollars are correct.

Metropolitan's short life yield program

The following was written by the staff of *Metropolitan Mortgage* and is reprinted with their permission. You will learn how to buy a note with maturity over 180 months but with the assumption that it will he paid off earlier.

This is a program designed to enhance your pay price on the "cream puff" transactions. If the transactions you are quoting meet the criteria of the short life *yield program, Metropolitan* allows you to calculate it as if there was a balloon in seven years (84 months).

Let's review the requirements followed by an example of how this benefits the broker.

Requirements for Qualifications:

- First position

- Owner occupied single-family residence.

- 6 months seasoning.

- Acceptable credit ("A" credit, as defined by *Metropolitan*, waives seasoning requirements).

- Acceptable appraisal equaling or exceeding sales price.

- Equity of 10% or more based on sales price.

- Remaining term 180 months or more.

Here is the original note with 355 payments remaining. Use the PV method to calculate the balance due.

Box #1: Calculate the PV

N	I/Y	PV	Pmt	FV
Payments Remaining on the note.	The face interest rate on the note.	Calculate the balance due on the note.	The payment amount as written on the note.	There is no balloon payment.
355	9	35,899.68	289.66	0
This is the original note the seller wished to sell.				

If we use the same yield rate, 12.5% to purchase the transaction (short life yield), *Metropolitan* would pay $30,200.85. This amounts to an additional $3,095.72 paid for this acquisition using the short life yield program.

What You Have Learned: The amortization remains at 355 months according to the stated terms in the note. Because a majority of these types of loans pay off early or the property sells within seven years, *Metropolitan* developed the short life yield program for acquisitions that fit the above mentioned requirements.

Note: Due to rounding differences, and answers within a few dollars are correct.

Metropolitan Mortgage needs a 12.5% yield. What would they pay for this note?

Box #2: Calculate the PV

N	I/Y'	PV	Pmt	FV
Payments remaining on the note.	*Metropolitan Mortgage's* yield.	Calculate the buy rate for this note	The calculated payment from Box #1 above.	There is no balloon payment written into this note.
355	12.5	27,105.13	289.66	0
The PV is what they will pay for this note.				

Here is an example to illustrate the effectiveness of *the short life yield program*. *Metropolitan Mortgage* allows you to assume the note will pay off in 84 months, You can add a fictitious balloon:

Box #3: Calculate the FV

N	I/Y	PV	Pmt	FV
This is an assumption that the note will be paid off in 54 months.	The face interest rate of the note.	The Present Value or *Balance due* on the note from Box #1.	This is the payment of the note.	Calculate the fictitious balloon payment.
84	9.0	-35,899.68	289.66	35,523.13
This is a new loan. but is only an assumption.				

The loan in Box #3 has no effect on the payer. It is just a way to increase the present value of the note to give the note seller more money. Statistics show that most long-term notes are paid off early and *Metropolitan Mortgage* is passing the potential savings on to the note seller and perhaps to you, the note brokers.

If we use a yield rate of 12.5% to purchase this transaction, *Metropolitan* would pay $30,200.85.

Box #4: Calculate the PV

N	I/Y	PV	Pmt	FV
This is an assumption that the note will be paid off in 84 months.	*Metropolitan Mortgage's* yield.	*Calculate the buy rate, for this* note.	The calculated payment from Box #1 above.	This is the fictitious balloon calculated in Box #3 above.
84	12.5	30,200.85	289.66	
The added balloon creates greater PV and more money for the note seller.				

Box #1: PV = $35,899.68

Box #2: PV = $27,105.13

Box #3: FV = $33,523.13

Box #4: PV = $30,200.85

Yields, Not Discounts

You will learn why and how to add a balloon payment to a note you are buying for some real profits.

A note with a Balloon Payment is worth more than a fully amortized note. That is why we seldom use the word "discount" when talking about the purchase price of a cash flow. The discount varies greatly with the length of the Payment stream. A fully amortizing 20-year note is worth much less today than a 30-year note with a 5-year Balloon Payment. Therefore, we don't talk about "discount," We talk about the "yield" we will earn on a note.

NOTE #1: FULLY AMORTIZED NOTE

Box #1: Clear your calculator. Calculate the Pmt

N	I/Y	PV	Pmt	FV
A 20-year note.	Face interest rate on the note.	The Balance due on the note.	Calculate the payment amount of the note.	There is no balloon payment.
240	10	-325.000	3,136.32	0
You are offered this note for possible purchase.				

Offer to buy this note to yield you 14%.

Box #2: Calculate the PV

N	I/Y	PV	Pmt	FV
A 20-year note.	Your required yield.	Calculate the amount you will pay for this note.	The payment amount from Box # 1.	There is no balloon payment.
240	14	252,212.94	3,136.32	0
The PV is what you will pay for this note to yield you 14%				

NOTE #2:   NOTE WITH A BALLOON

Let's add a balloon to the note. It is now an "interest only" note. Clear your calculator.

Box #3: Calculate the Pmt

N	I/Y	PV	Pmt	FV
Months until the balloon (FV) payment.	Face interest rate on the note.	The balance due on the note.	Calculate the payment amount of the note.	This is the balloon payment.
60	10	-325,000	2,708.33	325,000
This is an interest only loan. The payer is paying only "rent" (Pmt) on the $325,000 (PV) and must pay the full $325,000 (FV) in 60 months (N).				

Offer to buy this note to yield you 14%.

Box #4: Calculate the PV

N	I/Y	PV	Pmt	FV
Months until the balloon (FV) payment.	Your required yield.	Calculate the amount you will pay for this note.	The payment amount from Box #3.	This is the balloon payment.
60	14	278,441.57	2,708.33	325,000
The PV is what you will pay for this balloon note to yield you 14%.				

Amazing! The balloon note is worth $26,228.63 more than the fully amortizing note. To prove it, Subtract the PV from the balloon note in Box #4 from the PV of the amortizing note. Box #2 above.

NOTE #3: 20 DUE IN 5 NOTE

A variation is to create an amortizing note, but add a Balloon Payment. Commonly called a "20 due in 5" meaning a 20 year amortization, but with the balance all due and payable in 5 years. Here's an example of a "20 due in 5." It is a two-step process to create the original note.

Step 1

Box #5: Clear Your calculator. Calculate the Pmt

N	I/Y	PV	Pmt	FV
Assume this is a 20-year note.	Face interest rate on the note.	Amount owed on the note.	Calculate the payment as if this you were using an amortizing note.	There is no balloon payment yet.
240	10	-325,000	3,136.32	0
First find the Payment on the fully amortizing note.				

Now you need to add the Balloon Payment by changing the number of Payments (N) from 240 to 60 months (5 years).

Step 2

Box #6: Calculate the FV

N	I/Y	PV	Pmt	FV
Force the note to to be paid off in this many months.	Face interest rate on the note.	Amount owed on the note.	The payment as calculated in Box #5.	Calculate the Balloon due in 5 years.
60	10	-325,000	3,136.32	291,857.97
You now have a "20 due in 5" cash flow.				

What would you pay for this note to get a 14% yield?

Box #7: Calculate the PV

N	I/Y	PV	Pmt	FV
Balloon note.	Your required yield.	Calculate the amount you will pay for this note.	The payment as calculated in Box #5.	The balloon amount as calculated in Box #6.
60	14	280,310.49	3,136.32	291,857.90
The PV is the purchase price of this "20 due in 5" note.				

This last type of note allows the payer to pay down the note slightly, so they are facing a smaller Balloon Payment.

Comparison of Value $325,000

20 Year, Fully Amortized Note @ 14% is worth $291,857,97

Balloon Note due in 5 Years: $278,441.57

20 Due In 5 Years: $280,310.49

Note: The reason the "20 due in 5" is more valuable than the balloon note is that the Payments are larger.

What You Have Learned: If everything else is equal, a balloon note has a greater Present Value and is worth more than a note that is fully amortized. There are many ways to add a Balloon Payment to a Payment stream.

Box #1: Pmt = $3,136.32

Box #2: PV = $252,212.94

Box #3: Pmt = $2,708.33

Box #4: PV = $278,441.57

Box #5: Pmt = $3,136.32

Box #6: FV = $291,857.97

Box #7: PV = $280,310.49

Note: Due to rounding differences, answers within a few dollars are correct.

Balloons are not just for kids

You will learn the value and risks of a balloon note investment.

Have you considered buying only the balloon portion of an interest only note? It may seem somewhat risky and the profit may not be realized for many years. Nevertheless, in this time of uncertainty about the future of Social Security and pensions and the importance of starting to plan for your own retirement, buying balloons can be a great way to create your own pension plan. They may work well in a Roth IRA.

Box #1: Clear your calculator. Calculate the FV

N	I/Y	PV	Pmt	FV
60	12	-50.000	500	50,000
This is the original note.				

Box #2: Calculate the PV

N	I/Y	PV	Pmt	FV
Number of monthly payments you must wait for the balloon payment.	Your yield.	Calculate the price you can pay for this cash flow.	Payment is $0 because they will all go to the note seller.	The balloon amount you will receive in N months.
60	18	-20,464.80	0	50,000
PV is the discounted value today of a $50,000 balloon payment at I/Y in N months.				

Because of the time value of money, you can purchase the balloon portion of a note, for relatively little. A $50,000 balloon due in 5 years at 18% is only worth $20,464. As a partial purchase, the balloon only part does not seem to be as large a discount.

Consider the above note written at 12% interest only. Let's "up the ante." What would you pay for this whole note if you wanted a 20% yield?

Box #3: Calculate the PV

N	I/Y	PV	Pmt	FV
Number of payments you are buying.	Your yield	Calculate the price you will pay for this entire cash flow.	You will receive these payments.	You will receive this balloon payment
60	20	-37,418.48	500	50,000
PV is the price for the whole note.				

This is almost a 50% discount from the point of view of the seller and probably not acceptable. However, you can buy just the balloon (FV) and the discount disappears.

Box #4: Calculate the PV

N	I/Y	PV	Pmt	FV
Months you must wait for the balloon payment in FV.	Your yield	*Calculate what you would pay for the balloon (FV) in (N) months.*	The payments go to the note seller, not to you, the note buyers.	The balloon amount you will receive in N months.
60	20	-18,546.20	0	50,000
This is the value today of the balloon payment at a 20% yield.				

The seller gets $18,546.20 from you today, plus 60 payments of $500 or $30,000, for a total of $48,565.20. This is close to the face value of the note. The seller is happy because he perceives only a small discount.

What You Have Learned: Balloon only purchases don't take much cash and if you can make them safe, they can be a great investment for your IRA.

Box #1:   FV = - $50,000.00
Box #2:   PV = - $20,464.80
Box #3:   PV = - $37,418.48
Box #4:   PV = - $18,546.20

Note: Due to rounding differences, answers within a few dollars are correct.

Why do sellers sell balloon notes?

There are two reasons for selling the balloon for cash now from the seller's point of view:

(1) First, it seems like a long way off before any money will be actually received, and cash now might seem very inviting. Unlike monthly payments that might be missed, the balloon is just a promise of payment in the future. We live in a world of "instant gratification-I want it now!" The balloon is in the distant future (for many Americans, one year from now is the distant future).

(2) Second, there is the fear for many note holders that the payer won't be able to come up with the cash when the time is due. If the person couldn't qualify for a regular amortizing loan in the first place, what guarantee is there that he or she will qualify' for refinancing in the future, particularly if housing prices don't rise. This brings up the "F" word, you know, foreclosure.

This scares people who feel overwhelmed by the prospect of going through this process. Therefore, in your letters and post cards, in your newspaper ads and in your contacts with professional sources, why not let it be known that you can buy balloon only portions of notes as well as full and partial purchases. He or she will have the cash now to do with whatever is desired while ending the worry about whether the payer will be able to come up with money for this balloon when it is paid (desire and fear are certainly the two greatest motivators of human behavior).

As you accumulate money of your own to invest (including an IRA or some other kind of self-directed retirement account), you will find your money goes farther and at greater yields when you buy balloon payment notes. Remember that balloons often pay off early, thus greatly increasing your yield. Just turn around and reinvest it in a larger balloon note and watch your IRA grow.

Finally, it is very important to take control of the note although you are only buying the balloon portion. The seller must agree to give you recorded title to the mortgage. In a separate contract, you will agree to receive and distribute to the seller each monthly payment. This could even be done by a neutral third party, such as an escrow company or bank. This way you will know exactly when the balloon is to be paid off and will not have to go through the seller to make sure you receive it. Do not accept a deal in which you don't control the note and the cash flows.

If you do all the proper due diligence (appraisal, credit report, careful examination of all the documents, etc.), buying the balloon portion of the note can be a very profitable part of your note portfolio.

Partials

Partials have become quite popular in the discount mortgage industry in the last few years. They involve the purchase of a portion of a note instead of the entire note. The simplest form of partials is buying one cash flow out of a note that has two or more distinct cash flows.

Single cash flow purchase

A common example of this type of partial is where there is a note with monthly payments and then a balloon payment at a future date. Let's look at a $25,000 note with 8% interest and payments of $183.44 per month and a 60-month balloon.

To correspond with most calculators, the interest rate is shown as the periodic rate (monthly) instead of the annual rate.

N	I/Y	PV	Pmt	FV	
60	8	-25,000	183.44	23,767.55	Original Note
60	18	-23,767.46	183.44	16,951.89	Discounted to Yield 18%
60	18	-7,223.92	183.44	0	Payments only
60	18	0	183.44	17,649.62	Balloon only

An investor could buy the payments for $7,223.96 and let the seller keep the balloon. Another option for a partial would be to buy the balloon for $7,223.96 and let the seller keep the payments.

Divided cash flows

Partials can be structured by deciding how much of one or several cash flows to buy. For example, let's look at a 30-year amortization note.

N	I/Y	PV	Pmt	FV	
360	10	-10,000	87.76	0	Original Note
360	18	-5,822.97	87.76	0	Discounted to Yield 18%
180	18	-5,449.33	87.76	0	Purchase of ½ note at 18% Yield
90	18	-4,318.520	87.76	0	Purchase of ¼ of note (90 payments) at 18% Yield

It is interesting to note that there is only a $373.64 difference between the value of 30 years of payments and 15 years. A cash flow you begin to receive 15 years in the future just isn't worth very much.

One of the primary questions to ask a note seller is "How much cash do you need?" If their cash needs are low or they have a reality problem with how much a note is worth, then a partial is the ideal solution.

Full price partials

A "Full Price" partial is where we buy even portions of a note. A seller of a note unfamiliar with TVOM (the Time Value of Money) may view this method of partial in much more favorable terms. For example, lets say we buy one half of a $10,000 note for $5,000. If it is a thirty-year note and we buy the first fifteen years, we will have a great yield. It skyrockets if we buy one third or one fourth of the note.

N	I/Y	PV	Pmt	FV	
360	10	-10,000	87.76	0	Original Note
180	19.98	-5,000	87.76	0	½ note for ½ face amount
120	29.95	-3,333	87.76	0	1/3 of payments
90	39.91	-2,500	87.76	0	¼ of payments

The annual yields are: **19.98% for one half of the note.**

29.95% for one third of the note.

39.91% for one fourth of the note.

This is simpler for the note seller to understand

A rule of thumb is that the yield you receive will be the reciprocal of the percentage you buy multiplied by the interest rate. If I buy 1/3 of an 8% amortized note, I will receive a 24% rate of return. If I buy 1/3 of a 7% note, the yield will be 21%.

Alternate approaches

There are no set standard approaches in the industry and many different methods have been used.

The first approach (for buying one half of the note) is to buy the number of payments required to amortize the note down to $5,000. When the balance of the note is down to $5,000, the seller gets his payments back. This results in the seller receiving the last 78 payments. Your yield would be 20.9%.

The second approach is to leave the seller the last $5,000 worth of payments. The results would be the seller receiving the final 57 payments (57 times 87.76 = 5,000). Your yield would be 20.95%.

N	I/Y	PV	Pmt	FV	
360	10	-10,000	87.76	0	Original Note
282	20.90	-5,000	87.76	0	Purchase of 282 payments
303	20.95	-5,000	87.76	0	Yield when 303 payments are purchased
130	18.03	-5,000	87.76	0	18% Yield
180	19.98	-5,000	87.76	0	½ for ½

The last option shown is simple and makes the most sense for the seller of the note. Remember, **"A confused mind always says no."** Never get into the numbers with the note seller. They generally do not understand the time value of money. Don't talk yields with the note seller; it is contrary to the negotiation process.

Tall tails

How would you like $157,962.60 in profits on a $100,000 note that doesn't cost you anything to purchase? Would an extra $800 per month retirement interest you? How about doing it all tax-free (or deferred)?

This involves buying a whole note and then selling a partial to an investor or institution.

We buy a $100,000 note payable over 30 years at a 16% yield. Then we sell the first 15 years of payments at a slightly lower yield to recover the entire initial cash investment. We then end up keeping the last half of the note. We will receive the last 15 years of payments for no cash. Our net investment is negative $637.80, meaning we were paid to get half of a note for free.

N	I/Y	PV	Pmt	FV	
360	10	-100,000	877.57	0	Original Note
360	16	-65,258.63	877.57	0	Discounted to 16%
180	14	-65,896.55	877.57	0	180 payments at 14% Yield
N/A	??	-637.92	N/A	0	Buying whole note and selling off half.

You will receive the last 15 years worth of payments on the "tail" end of the note. The total of payments you will receive is $157,962.60.

Tax free tails

How do you do it and minimize tax liabilities? Many people do not realize they can buy and sell notes using their IRA or other pension plan. All IRAs are self-directed and you can choose a cooperative trustee to assist your prudent paper investment.

Notes:

Staged Funding
Multiple partials

You can use what might be termed "multiple partials" or "Staged funding." Using the previous examples, imagine buying the first half of a 30 year note and then the other half 15 years later. If the yield is 20% by buying the first half of the note, then the yield will also be 20% when I buy the next half 15 years later.

As an example, you buy half of a 30-year $10,000 note for $5,000 now and then 15 years from now you pay $5,000 for the second half of the note. This can be structured as an option or scheduled as a purchase. If scheduled as a purchase, it can be done contractually or with a note secured by the note being purchased or some other collateral.

This can lead to some very creative scenarios like buying one tenth of a ten-year note each year. Each year one tenth of the price is paid. There will be a total of ten payments to the note seller. One now and then one each year for 9 years.

N	I/Y	PV	Pmt	FV	
120	10	-10,000	132.15	0	Original Note
120	18	-7,334.16	132.15	0	Value at 18% Yield
12	95.04	-1,000	132.15	0	Buying 12 payments per year for $1,000
Same each year	95.04				Annualized yield of 95.04%

Benefit-structured partials

Partials can be structured to meet various needs of the seller. For example, let's say the seller has a $50,000 note with payments per month of $500 at 10% for 216 months. The seller needs $20,000 now and $5,000 per year to help defray expenses for a child in college. We could give him $5,000 for 5 years and have a 15.61% yield.

To do these calculations, you need to use the irregular cash flow features of the calculator. Many older or inexpensive calculators or computer programs cannot deal with uneven cash flows.

The first column shows the cash flow number. The calculator assumes that they are consecutive, so if there were a period with no payments, you would schedule it as a cash flow of zero amount.

The second column shows the amount of the cash flow. The first cash flow or cash flow zero is the amount invested at time zero (today). A negative number is an amount I, as the investor, pay; a positive number is the amount I, as the investor, receive. In this case, the initial cash flow (CFO) is —20,000 because that is what the seller needs today.

The third column is the number of times a cash flow is received. After making the purchase, there will be monthly payments of $500 received until month twelve when a $5,000 payment is due. That same month, there will be an offsetting $500 making a net investment of $-4,500 in month twelve.

After the periodic cash flows are all entered in, you can solve for IRR or the initial rate of return. This will be a periodic amount that needs to be multiplied by twelve in this case to achieve an annual yield.

If you make a mistake in entering the cash flows, you will need to re-enter the cash flows again to make sure they are correct.

Periodic Cash Flow Example for Benefit Structured Partials

#	Cash Flow	# Times
0	-20,000	1
1	500	11
2	-4,500	1
3	500	11
4	-4,500	1
5	500	11
6	-4,500	1
7	500	11
8	-4,500	1
9	500	11
10	-4,500	1

| | 11 | 500 | 156 | |

IRR= 1.30 Periodic or 15.61 annual

The way we arrived at 5 years was just through experimentation. This would give the seller of the note a total of $45,000 for his or her $50,000 present balance. Remember, the yearly figure shows as 4,500 instead of $5,000 since there is an off-setting payment of $500 received in those months.

Now that you see some of the flexibility, you can structure notes as many ways as your mind can imagine.

When you have the flexibility and tools to meet the seller's needs in a win-win situation, you can buy as many notes as you need.

Amortized partials

Another partial technique to use is an "amortized partial." An amortized partial is where there is a series of payments over regular intervals. The most common form of amortized partial is to have a monthly payment for a set number of months.

Let's look at the example of a $50,000 note. The note is purchased with payments of $500 per month for 216 months at 10% interest. We will purchase it with an amortized partial of $50,000 payable $1,000 per month for 50 months.

When discounted to a 15% yield, this note would be worth $37,263.21 in cash today, but we are going to buy it with payments. Instead of a discounted amount, the seller of the note will receive 50 monthly payments of $1,000. There are numerous benefits to this approach and situations where it is the ultimate win-win scenario.

N	I/Y	PV	Pmt	FV
216	10	-50,000	500	0
216	15	-37,266.41	500	0
50	0	-50,000	1,000	0
50	10	-40,754.42	1,000	
41.34	6	-37,263.21	1,000	

Line one shows the note being purchased.

Line two shows this note's value at a 15% yield.

Line three shows the "amortized partial" purchase note.

Line four shows the value of the 50 payments at a 10% yield.

Line five shows the cash value of the mortgage invested at 6% yield.

Line four illustrates the type of return the seller is getting. It is much better than cash and the available yields for that cash.

Line five illustrates the type of reinvestment rate possible if the cash were invested. Our offer is a much better deal for a seller who needs more cash flow.

Notes:

_____

_____

_____

_____

_____

_____

_____

_____

Risks and rewards of partials and staged funding

The Rewards

Negotiation Power

The ability to structure more palatable win-win offers for a note seller is a tremendous advantage. As we focus on the seller's note, our odds of success are much higher. Competition is reduced because the other note buyers just offer cash at a large discount, which many times does not suit the seller's needs.

A seller that sees and knows that you are concerned about meeting their needs is also a lot more likely to sell to you.

The extreme discounts are avoided or minimized by partials and the resulting emotions that they cause the seller of the note.

The average note seller does not understand the time value of money, never wants to, and never will. Even if you teach them why their note is discounted, they would disagree.

Widening Your Market

Through the use of partials, we can capture much of the market that would sell under better terms than a large discount for cash. This makes it possible for you to reach past the area of people who "need to sell" into the area where people would sell a note if the benefits work for them.

The amortized partial reaches a group of people who need or could use a larger monthly cash flow. This is a huge market.

Increased Yields

Many times you can increase your yield substantially with the use of partials. Most MBA's couldn't figure the yield, let alone the average note seller. They just know their needs are met.

Cash Flow Re-Investment – A True IRR Solution

Few people can figure the yield or IRR on a note. The correct use of partials, in particular amortized partials, can substantially boost the yield on your entire portfolio.

The problem with IRR is that it assumes cash flow is re-invested at the same rate of return as you are receiving. If your calculator says you are getting an 18% yield that is accurate only if it is a single payment note or you are re-investing the monthly payment at 18% each month.

In the amortized partial that we used as an example, you would be investing $500 each month for 50 months. This would be a good place to place the funds from a note (or notes) where you are receiving $500 per month.

A few amortized partials can help get the funds of a note portfolio re-invested rapidly at a high yield.

An exciting advantage is that it opens an avenue of note investment for the investor or individual who has excess cash flow to invest, but not a large lump sum. The young professional can start investing earlier. IRA's and other retirement funds are a good source.

Potential risks of partials

Foreclosure or Bankruptcy

When you buy a partial, there are two parties involved if there is a default, foreclosure, or bankruptcy in the future. The way most people structure partials is very dangerous. They are entering into a quasi-partnership with the note seller. Usually the note seller has little knowledge of what is going on, which results in lawsuits.

If you use the "contractual" method of a partial, you need to address who is in charge, who pays what costs, what the rights of all parties are, and how the note seller can protect himself in the case of default. Before doing a partial using this method, consult your attorney.

Early Payoff

The same problems of joint ownership stated above come into play here. If there is an early payoff, who gets what? This has to be spelled out in detail at the time the note is purchased.

If the "contractual" method is used, much of the profit incentive is gone. Early payoffs are great, yet the way most people structure partials make an early payoff unattractive. They build a generous reward for themselves into the deal, but the note seller balks many times when it is high.

Insolvency or Financial Problems

Any joint ownership of the note can also lead to problems that need to be addressed or avoided relating to the note seller's financial status. If the seller files bankruptcy, a "contractual" structure on a partial may be considered a loan by the court and you could be at risk of losing your collateral (when using the "contractual" method).

Lender Liability

At least one court has considered the "contractual" method of a partial as a loan to the seller instead of a purchase. Some brokers attempt to protect themselves by having the seller sign a document stating that it is not a loan.

To use a common analogy, if it looks like a duck, walks like a duck and has feathers like a duck-it may not make much of a difference if the seller signs a statement saying it isn't a duck. Ongoing legal research suggests that a partial done in the "contractual" manner is a loan.

If you run the liability of a partial being construed as a loan, you may come under lending laws like:

Regulation Z

Reg. Z is a federal law with requirements such as spelling out the APR (Annual Percentage Rate), and in some cases offering a right of rescission.

Usury

Local state usury laws would apply and the yields you are receiving may violate usury limits.

Mortgage Lending Regulations

There are both state and federal laws relating to lending money. In some states, there is licensing or bonding required. Other states have disclosure laws and their own versions of Regulation Z.

How to Structure a Partial

There are three ways to structure the form and paperwork relative to partials. There are some distinct advantages and disadvantages to each form. The first form is the one most commonly used and has the most disadvantages. It is the most common because some of the institutions use this format. The least common is the "compensating note" structure.

1-Contractual

This method of structuring a partial involves a form of joint ownership and spells out the interests of both parties. The note is assigned to the purchaser and then re-assigned to the original seller at the end of a certain term. The advantages are that it can be easier to structure for an institution, but can be very costly later if the partial is construed as a loan. Note sellers seldom understand their rights, liabilities, and responsibilities.

2 -Note Splitting

Another technique is to actually split the note into two (or more) notes. The seller can take a subordinated interest. For example, you split a first mortgage into a first and a second. Squeeze the payments into the first and have the second begin paying when the first is fully paid off. The payer would need to be brought into the picture and possibly compensated or enticed in some manner. Still, this may be a much better option than the contractual agreement method. It is better to solicit the payer's cooperation now than try and deal with the potential problems of the failed contract method.

3-Compensating Note

This requires buying the "Whole" note, not just a partial. The terms look the same and the yield is comparable or better. You pay part cash and give the note seller a newly created note for the balance. It mirrors or reflects the portion of the note that I am not paying cash for. To buy a $10,000 10 year note, you pay $5,000 cash and give the seller a $5,000 note that begins payments in 5 years.

The note you buy is: $10,000 at 10% interest payable at $132.15 per month for 10 years (120 months).

You want to buy one half of the note or 60 payments for $5,000. The last 60 payments will be reflected in a $5,000 note to the note seller. It is structured with no payments for 60 months and then will begin payments and totally amortize in months 61 through 120.

Where's the Security?

This note that you give the seller can be unsecured or secured by any type of collateral. I can use other real estate equities, another note, personal property, or even the note you are buying.

Notes:

_____

_____

_____

_____

_____

_____

_____

_____

Staged Funding for Risk Management

**Notice — This is not meant to cover the entire subject of risk management, only to give a few examples of how partials can aid in covering hidden risks, minimizing foreclosure risk and facilitate faster closings.

One of the most powerful uses of staged funding is in the area of risk management. It has been used for a time in a few areas like adjusting investment to value ratios, but most investors do not use partials for much more than that.

Adjusting the ITV

Most investors invest solely based on LTV's or "Loan to Value" ratios. Many investors look at the ratio, which has taken on the term ITV or "Investment to Value" ratio.

This ratio differs in that it takes into account not the full amount of the note you are buying, but the discounted amount you pay. With discounted mortgages, the loan to value ratio may look horrible while the investment to value ratio looks great. Here's an example:

Investment to value illustration

We are buying a first mortgage note of $95,000 on a property with a current value of $100,000. This would equal an LTV ratio of 95%. This would exceed most note investors acceptable LTV ratios which are usually 80% as the maximum.

What if we could purchase this note for $60,000? The ITV ratio would be only 60%. A total of $60,000 is invested and it is secured by $100,000 in property value. This would be a very safe investment even though the LTV is not acceptable. For this reason, many investors now have dual criteria where either a good LTV or a good ITV would be acceptable.

Partials can be used to adjust the ITV. You can work backwards from the ITV to the amount you can give in cash. In the previous example, let's say that the $95,000 note is worth $90,000. This is the amount we would pay if there were acceptable LTV ratios.

If your requirements are an 80% LTV or a 70% ITV, then you could not justify purchasing this mortgage for all cash. That would equal a 95% LTV and a 90% ITV.

You can work backwards and structure a partial where you give the note seller $70,000 or less and arrange a partial in one of the manners described previously. In a case like this one, you would want it to be real clear that the seller's interest is subordinated to yours.

You would give the seller $70,000 cash and a $25,000 note. If there are any problems, like foreclosure, their note does not get paid until after yours is paid in full.

Contingency hold backs

A "Contingent" partial can be used to cover such items as:

1-Liens, Loans or Judgments that need to be cleared.

Most monetary items or other items affecting the title can be quantified to an amount that can be held back or structured as a contingent partial. Hold back 200% of the amount if that is what it takes to feel comfortable. If the partial is contingent, then payment can occur when and if the problems are solved.

2-Repairs, Upgrades, Rehab, or Maintenance Items.

Improvements to the collateral can be structured just as any other monetary items. If the property is being rehabilitated, or needs repair, you can hold back sufficient funds to fund the repairs or complete the rehab.

3-Payment and/or Tax Reserve

In many cases, you may want to hold back a certain number of payments. You can hold these payments back from the seller's funds as security. This is true in cases where the payer has been behind in payments in the past or in some other way has been delinquent about paying (*do not tell the payer about the funds held back). If you or your investor has a need for the monthly cash flow, then plan it out. "Pre-paid" payments can also serve to upgrade the note and improve the payment history in some cases.

All details on any hold back or partial agreements relating to the above items should be spelled our clearly and reviewed with an attorney. Many of these items can also be covered under the concept described called "Worst Case" funding.

The consolidation partial

A more advanced form of staged funding using partials would be where the payer has poor credit, a bad debt structure, and poor ability to pay on the loan. How could you do anything in a case like that?

Use a form of partial where the note is purchased from the note seller with part cash and a subordinated note. Some of the cash goes to the payer to clean up his debts, adjust his debt structure, and improve his ability to pay the loan. A loan subordinate to the note you are buying is created from the payer to the note seller as his "partial."

Putting partials into practice

Who To Market To

Partials and staged funding work very well for individuals who don't want to take a large discount, don't need all of their cash now, need a greater cash flow, or cases where a note is not acceptable for an all cash purchase.

How To Market Staged Funding

Adapt your advertising by mentioning that you can pay higher prices for notes or even full price. Ads that state no discount or "Full price" for notes will help get the calls and open the door. Adapt your flyers, brochures and sales pitches to agents to include the ability to structure a win-win deal that meets the seller's needs.

Adapt your negotiations by opening the door to partials and listening carefully to the seller's needs. He or she does not necessarily need all cash, or in some cases, any cash. As you explore their needs, you may learn there are better options. You may find you can out bid your stiffest competitors by paying a higher price using a partial-and still get your higher yield.

Explore target markets like nursing homes, social security administration, and probate courts. Nursing homes may have residents or potential residents that have notes and need cash – or greater cash flow (like an amortized partial).

Securing Your Funding

Learn about existing funding sources that already have funds to buy partials. Become familiar with their forms, requirements and policies. Know who to go to and what they can offer you.

Cultivate investors in your local area that understand partials and have cash, cash flow, borrowing power, and/or real estate equities as a resource to buy notes and put together staged funding situations. Few investors will understand partials, and you may need to carefully educate them.

Negotiating a Partial

The first key to negotiation of a partial is to fully understand and be fluent in the potential options. Practice with the calculator and constantly run through the different scenarios. You will know you understand it when you start seeing new applications for the techniques. When you understand them well enough to teach them to someone else, then you are ready.

The next step is to practice asking the questions and role-playing. It can be very valuable to have someone develop a sample note and run through a sample phone conversation with you.

Defer to a more experienced negotiator. A good negotiator can save you far more then they ever charge you.

The Sale Leaseback With a New Twist

Today, the interest rates on real estate remain at all time lows and finding notes to buy as a broker is harder than it use to be. On the other hand, there are literally tens of thousands of homeowners in the mist of a financial crisis. Unfortunately, accessing the value of their home equity is difficult and impossible for many of these same people since their credit history often precludes them from raising cash by borrowing against the property.

A possible solution to this problem is a relatively new twist to the old sell/leaseback option, where people need a lump sum of cash and for one reason or another cannot acquire the funds from a traditional bank or mortgage company. The reasons vary. They might have insufficient credit, and as you know, most decisions to make a loan today are based on credit scores. Their credit may be okay, but there are certain elements of the borrower's background that increase the lenders perceived risk that they do not fit the lenders profile. Some of these include self-employment, a new job, new in their profession, or limited time in the area, or a past bankruptcy, and/or too much debt, which prevents them from obtaining a mortgage. Most mortgage underwriters work against a series of preconceived formulas. People, who do not fit, are said to be out of the formula.

It is interesting to note that lenders do not make real estate loans. They make credit loans secured by real estate.

Our emphasis is in investing in real estate and not making anyone a loan.

To illustrate this point, let's take the example of a rental house that is offered to you for sale. It's a good house but the landlord just can't seem to get a tenant who will stay in very long, or the one they have now is very slow paying and will probably have to be dispossessed at some time in the future. The owner of the rental property is very anxious to sell.

Here is how the program works. If a homeowner decides to sell us his or her property at 60% to 70% of it's realistic market value, we now have a few problems, but the risk of loss is very low. You may agree that this is very possible but who in their right mind would do such a thing. The answer is people looking for money who can't get financing and who do not want to move from their residence. Once this program is explained, it is an attractive idea because we can get the funds they want, at a payment (rent) they agree they can afford, and they retain an option to repurchase the property at the very same price they sold it , **OR EVEN LESS**.

You can earn tax-deferred income up front, cash flow from the rent for a period of years, and an additional back end cash flow when the property is repurchased or the lease defaults.

If you need quick cash, can't you can sell some real estate you own at a real bargain? There are always bargain hunters. So far so good. But then you would take a beating on the value, and if it were your residence, you would have to move out. But, what if you could continue living in your house and after 13 or 16 months, buy it back for the same price that you sold it, and then in some cases, less.

Please understand that we're not discussing a loan. **WE DON'T LOAN MONEY. WE BUY REAL ESTATE AND LEASE IT BACK**. We would buy it at about 60%-70% of the appraised value as an owner occupied single-family residence.

An existing home loan must be paid off as part of the transaction. If the owner wants to continue to live in the house, we lease it back to him and give him an option to buy it back from us at a set price in as little as 13 months. Our longest time frame is 60 months. In the event that the owner does not want to continue living in the house, then he would have the right to sublease it to a new tenet. However, we would look to him for the monthly payment.

But what if his credit is bad because of a divorce, being out of work for 2 months, a recently discharged bankruptcy? It doesn't matter. If you can show that he has the income to make the rent payments on time, we will look at the property we are buying and not his credit.

What are the risks for the seller? There are several major areas of risks. First, if he doesn't pay the rent on time, in addition to a late charge, he does not receive any rent credit for that month against the option price. Second, consistent late payments or skipped payments are reason for us to cancel the option. He can buy the house at the end of the lease, but it would be at the full fair market value. Thirdly, a poor rent payment history can also result in default under the lease. The lease must be kept current in order to retain the option on the house. And finally, he must exercise his option not later than the end of the option period (minimum 13 months-depending on the amount involved and a maximum 60 months). Generally, this whole program takes about 10 days with a maximum of 30 days.

STEP 1.

Determine the purchase price. To some extent this will depend on the client's needs. We use 60% to 70% of the value as a maximum. But if the client had a $75,000 property and only needed $25,000, we would be glad to purchase the property for a third of its value. Wouldn't we have an extremely safe investment? Since the rent is based on the purchase price, do you think the Seller/Tenant would forfeit the home by not keeping the lease payment current?

On the other hand, if 70% is the maximum investment to value and the loan balance was $35,000.00 on the $75,000.00 property, your owner could only receive $17,500.00 before expenses [$75,000 x 70% = $52,500.00-$35,000.00 = $17,500]. In spite of this, the lease back would be based on $52,500.00.

Any expenses of acquiring the property (legal fees, title policy, escrow fees, etc.) come out of the Seller's pocket.

Purchase Price $_____

A.   Estimated Monthly Taxes $_____

Remember homeowners sometimes get certain deductions. After you purchase it, the seller will not have any deductions.

B.   Estimated Monthly Ins. $_____

Purchase only fire and extended coverage insurance. The Seller/Tenant should buy a Tenant policy to protect their personal property.

C.   Agreed Monthly Rent $_____

TOTAL LEASE BACK FEE (A+B+C) $

STEP 2

Using only "C", above play "what if' with your calculator to calculate a satisfactory cash flow. You should have some idea what the client thinks they can afford or is willing to pay for rent from the initial contact conversation. If they want low rent, then you can only pay so much for the property. You may have to say, "I cannot give you what you need in the way of cash, unless you can pay X amount of monthly rent." The calculator might give you a number with Dollars and Cents. ALWAYS ROUND THE RENT UP TO A WHOLE NUMBER, since rent is never an uneven number. Remember WE ARE NOT LENDING MONEY, WE ARE INVESTING IN REAL ESTATE IN SUCH A WAY THAT WE HAVE A MINIMUM OF MANAGEMENT PROBLEMS.

STEP 3

Once you have reached an agreement with the client, recalculate the deal to present to an investor. Depending on the collateral, yields to the Investor in a range of 9% to 12.5% should enable you to attract the money to do the deal. We base our offers to investors on a spread above New York Prime. At this writing, we pay between 3.5% to 6% over prime.

Your goal is to create a spread on the front end, collect a portion of the rent, and to receive an option price that is more than you will owe the investor on his loan to you. Thus, you get three bites at the apple. See the attached sample. You should prepare an Amortization schedule showing the Investor what the Investment will produce for him. In addition, we use an appraisal and a credit report. Credit is important. However, you should satisfy yourself that the Seller/Tenant has enough income to pay the rent.

STEP 4

You will need the following documents:

1. Purchase offer signed by both parties. If the seller has a real estate agent he/she can write the agreement. If not, use an attorney to write a simple cash offer. There should also be an addendum to the contract informing the Seller/Tenant that is was not the intention of any party to create a mortgage or a mortgagor/mortgagee relationship.

2. Lease agreement

While the "C" amount remains constant over the terms of the lease, escalators for taxes and insurance should be built into the lease.

3. Option agreement

DO NOT COMBINE THE LEASE AND OPTION AGREEMENTS IN THE SAME DOCUMENT.

4. Note and Mortgage to the Investor

We never sign personally. It is not necessary. The investor must understand that he/she must look to the real estate in the event of default on the lease.

5. Title Insurance is an absolute must.

6. Property Tax certificate. Any unpaid taxes must be paid from the proceeds of the sale.

7. Release of any prior liens, judgments, etc.

CHECK WITH YOUR LEGAL ADVISOR!

Let's assume a homeowner who needs cash approaches you.

Here is a typical situation:

1. A free and clear property. Value as determined by an appraisal is $74,900.

2. Seller/Tenant feels $750 per month including taxes and insurance is all they can pay.

3. Taxes for an investment property will be $1,865 per year, $155.42 per month (rounded $160).

4. Insurance fire and extended coverage is $950 per year, or $79.17 per month (rounded $80).

5. $750 – 160 – 80 = $510 per month.

6. Seller/Tenant would like $45,000

Remember PV is the purchase price of the property; FV is the Option Price at the end of the Lease.

Let's play "What If' with our calculators

N	I/Y	PV	PMT	FV
36	?	-45,000	510	42,000

N	I/Y	PV	PMT	FV
36	11.74	-45,000	510	42,000

Not bad, but nowhere near our goal of an 18% return. Let's change the rate of return to 18 and re-solve for the purchase price.

N	I/Y	PV	PMT	FV
36	18.00	-38,680	510	42,000

Well, this is not working. Part of the mystique of the deal is the promise that the Seller/Tenant can buy the property back for LESS THAN THEY SOLD IT FOR! We try and use a reduction of about $1,000 per year or 2% of the original purchase price, whichever is greater. The Seller/Tenant is adamant they cannot pay anymore than $510. Let's reduce the amount of the purchase and lengthen the deal by one year to 48 months.

N	I/Y	PV	PMT	FV
48	17.49	-31,000	510	27,000

Pretty close, actually to get exactly 18%, the Rent would have to be $522.50 (round down to $520) if you get that close, and $31,000 solves the problem. They will pay the extra $10. You could also increase the option price by allowing them less than $1,000 per year and keep the rent at $510 per month.

N	I/Y	PV	PMT	FV
48	18.00	-31,000	510	27,900

Let's say the seller/tenant) agrees to the deal presented above, and you have an investor who will lend you money without personal liability for 10.5% return. You decide you want to make $2,000 on the back end of the deal, and $60 per month during the deal. Let's see what the investor will pay for the income stream you create.

	N	I/Y	PV	PMT	FV
Seller/Tenant	48	18.00	-31,000	510	27,869.57
Investor	48	10.52	-34,600	450	25,900
YOU	48		3,600	60	2,000

You can make a total of $8,480 during the course of the deal. The $3,600 is a non-taxable event because it is borrowed money. The $60 is partially off set by the interest on the loan from the investor, and it is possible that the $27,900 resale price could be considered a loss since the original basis was $31,000.

In the unlikely event the seller/lessee defaults on the lease and loses his/her option, you can sell the property again. In that event we would share the profit after all expenses, including a realtor commission, with the investor.

Provide an option printout to the seller/lessee. Put an early pay-off penalty in the schedule for the first 22 months in order to cover the front-end premium. In the above case, the first month pay-off would be $34,600. The penalty disappears after 22 months and is reduced to the $27,900 option price at the 48th month. Another alternative is to reduce the front-end premium and net more per month from the rent. .

	N	I/Y	PV	PMT	FV
Investor	48	10.52	-31,000	357.68	25,900

Or $1,500 front end

	N	I/Y	PV	PMT	FV
Investor	48	10.52	-32,500	396.10	25,900

You can make $152.32 per month ($510 - $357.68) instead of $60 with no premium, or $113.90 ($510 - $396.10) with $1,500 premium and still have the back end bonus of $2,000. In the above example he made a total of $48,480, with $1,500 on the front end, the total of $8,967.07. With no premium, the gross is $9,311.21. Play "what if" until you find a combination that works for you.

What if the seller/lessee was adamant about receiving $45,000 and agreed he could pay more rent. How much would he have to pay, and what could you make?

N	I/Y	PV	PMT	FV
48	18.00	-45,000	732.50	41,000

Round down the rent to $730, plus $160, plus $80 for a total of $970.

N	I/Y	PV	PMT	FV
48	17.93	-45,000	730	41,000

	N	I/Y	PV	PMT	FV
Investor	48	10.57	-49,000	600	39,000

OUTSTANDING! $4,000 on the front end, $130 per month and $2,000 on the back end. TOTAL= $12,240

This is a win-win-win for everyone:

WIN-1   Investor gets a safe management free real estate loan investment with a good return and a chance for an even larger return in the event of default.

WIN-2 The Seller/Lessee (Tenant) finds the money he needs to solve his problems. He does not have to move with the trauma that entails and if he exercises the option or sell the property at fair market value later, he does not suffer any loss.

WIN-3   You make money and render a unique service to another individual.

How to lower your house payment

You can borrow some of the equity out of a house and invest it at a higher rate of return than it was borrowed, and create a nice cash flow. Some people would use a debt consolidation loan, and simply stretch out the inevitable, thereby compounding the problem. There is a better way. Example:

BEFORE		AFTER
$100,000	Value	$100,000
$20,000	Loan Balance	$80,000
$587.01	Payment	$479.64
$0	Payment Difference	$107.37
8.0%	Interest Rate	6.0%
$0 ($60,000 @ 24% @120mos.)	Income at 24%	$1,322.89
$0	Cash Flow Difference	$843.25 (For 120 mos.)

Before restructuring the house mortgage, there was an outgo of $587.01. After the re-structure and investing in a mortgage or mortgages yielding 24%, there is a positive cash flow of $843.25 per month for 120 months. AND NO HOUSE PAYMENT! You could use this extra cash for additional investments or wine, women, and song. However there is a better way.

Pay off the mortgage early

Instead of spending the excess on wine, women, and song, use it to pay off the mortgage early. Suppose you applied all of the $843.25 cash flow difference towards the mortgage payment. What would be the effect? The $1,322.89 per month generated from the purchase of the mortgage yielding 24% applied to a $80,000 loan balance at 6% interest amortized over 360 months would be paid off in 52.97 months or 4.41 years. There would still be a cash flow of $88,633.33 left which is payable over a period of the remaining 67 months. You have just turned your mortgage debt into a cash flow investment machine. Having a paid for house in just under five years is just your production bonus for using a little bit of investment savvy.

Notes:

Get even richer by building your net worth

When you buy paper at a discount, the FACE AMOUNT of the paper shows up as an asset on your financial statement, not what you paid for it. If you borrow against the paper, you are borrowing against the face value of the note.

Popping balloons for peace of mind

We have seen by our previous example that by increasing the payment on the note that the amortization can be greatly reduced, and a balloon payment can be eliminated entirely. This can be a win-win situation for both the party paying on the note and the party receiving the payments. If a party is paying on a note, the security and peace of mind of not having to worry about the balloon payment is well worth the gradual payment increase, and might make the property more saleable. For example, a $10,000 note bearing interest at 10% with a 30-year amortization would have a payment of $87.76 per month. If this note had a five-year balloon, the amount due in five years would be $9,657.43.

If the payment graduated just $30 per month, how long would it take to pay the loan off? The first step is to figure the amount of the principal balance after the first year of payments. The new balance is brought down to the next line, the interest rate stays the same, but the payment is increased, and the calculator solves for how long the loan would take to amortize. The balance after one year's worth of payments is then calculated and brought down to the next line, the payment is increased again, and etc.

$30/MO. PER YEAR GRADUATION TO POP A 5 YEAR BALLOON

I/Y	PMT	PV	FV	N
10	87.76	-10,000	N/A	360.00
10	117.76	-10,000	N/A	148.20
10	147.76	-9,567.45	N/A	93.46
10	177.76	-8,712.59	N/A	63.36
10	207.76	-7,391.26	N/A	42.37
10	237.76	-5,554.60	N/A	26.09
10	113.80	-113.80	N/A	1

* * * Make sure you clear the calculator and re-enter the numbers each time

Increasing the payment-$50 increments

The Original Note: $10,000 (PV), 180 payments (N), 10% (I/Y), monthly payment $107.46 (Pmt)

N	I/Y	PV	PMT	FV
180	10	10,000	107.46	19,342.80
90.78	10	10,000	157.46	14,294.22
62.89	10	10,000	207.46	12,839.70
41.13	10	10,000	257.46	12.134.09

The loan will be paid off more quickly, and the payer will save a lot of money. THE SAVINGS:

INCREASE	SAVES	PAYS LOAN OFF
$ 50 mo.	$5,048.58	7.4 years earlier
$100 mo.	$6,503.10	9.8 years earlier
$150 mo.	$7,208.71	11.1 years earlier

What does this do to the yield and value of the note? The FV column below is the value that the note would have at the yield it was bought at (24%), and the I/Y column is the new yield on the note, based on what we paid for it.

Increased payment, yield, and value

N	I/Y	PV	PMT	FV
180	24	5,220.88	107.46	10,000.00
90.78	33.14	5,220.88	157.46	6,568.58
62.89	42.02	5,220.88	207.46	7,327.63
41.13	50.79	5,220.88	257.46	7,810.63

To realize an immediate profit, you could resell the note at the higher value shown above and realize the profit shown below. A better option would be to sell a partial interest in the note or to obtain a loan against it.

Increase in payment	Increase in value
$ 50	$1,347.70
$100	$2,106.75
$150	$2,589.00

Offer to lower the interest for a higher payment

If the payer is still not convinced that he should increase his payments, then make him the following offer. Offer to reduce the interest if he will increase the payments. We will have to give up a little of our profit, but at these yields it won't hurt too bad. If we lower the interest rate, the payer will save even more money and will be more inclined to agree to the change. Our yield will still increase tremendously. In our example below, we will lower the interest rate 2% for every $50 increase in the monthly payment. How much you decrease the interest rate and increase the payment is all a matter of negotiation. The first line below is the original note. The payment total is shown in the FV column.

N	I/Y	PV	PMT	FV
180	10	10,000	107.46	19,342.80
82.86	8	10,000	157.46	13,047.14
55.29	6	10,000	207.46	11,470.76
41.67	4	10,000	257.46	10,728.00

The new yield

You would increase your yield tremendously. In the following example, we will examine the differences in yield as well as the differences in the value of the note. As a result of this increase in yield and value, an investor could "flip" the note again for a quick profit. The new value of the note is shown in the FV column.

N	I/Y	PV	PMT	FV
82.68	32.1	5,220.88	157.46	6,347.09
55.29	39.8	5,220.88	207.46	6,902.43
41.67	47.4	5,220.88	257.46	7,232.59

Notes:

Converting long term paper to short term paper

You can use these same principles to convert long term paper into short term paper, even though the yield increase is not substantial. This will enable you to increase your cash flow and make your paper more sellable or loanable. Look at the following example. If we double the payment on the note and reduce the interest rate to zero (0%) percent, this would shorten the term of the note from ten (10) years to just over three (3) years. Our yield would increase to 35%.

N	I/Y	PV	PMT	FV
120	10	-10,000	132.15	N/A - original note
37.84	0	-10,000	264.30	N/A – original note
120	24	-5,993.71	132.15	Cost of note
37.84	35.19	-5,993.71	264.30	Yield at 0$

Notes:

_____

_____

_____

_____

_____

_____

_____

_____

Notes:

Using paper to buy real estate

One of the most exciting and profitable aspects of discounted notes and mortgages is the different creative techniques one can utilize in buying real estate. The value of paper varies from person to person and changes with the economy. There is no secondary market where you can sell privately held notes and mortgages like Fannie Mae, Ginny Mae, and Freddie Mac. Therefore the value fluctuates from individual to individual. To most people, the value of paper is the face value. As we now know, this is not true. A great many people will accept a $25,000 note at face value, even though you may have bought it for $13,757.15.

Whenever a seller sells his real estate and agrees to take back a note and mortgage, he is in effect agreeing in effect to discount the value of his property, even though he might not realize it. Most people do not fully understand the concept of present value, and cannot see that they are discounting their property by taking paper in exchange for part of their equity.

Buying paper at a discount and trading it at face value to someone for their real estate can create tremendous profits. This can be done both with real and personal property. When this occurs, the discount is immediately realized in the property. Even though the seller may receive full price for his property, he just sold it for a discount.

Example:

The seller sells a parcel of real estate for $100,000. For purposes of simplicity, let's assume there was no down payment and the property is free and clear, and the seller is willing to take back a note for $100,000. If we were to buy a $100,000 note on a different property for $60,000 and trade it to our seller for full face value ($100,000), we would have effectively bought the seller's property for $60,000. (A 40% discount). Could you not then go to the mortgage company and get a loan on the property that you now own for 80% LTV., pay the seller of the note the $60,000 owed on the note at closing, and put $20,000 in HIP National Bank? Could this not be done at a simultaneous closing? Are You Awake Yet?

Realistically, properties do not all sell for no money down, and they are not all free and clear, and you can't always find a note that exactly matches the seller's needs. But, if you understand this concept of substitution of collateral, the possibilities are endless of what you can do to acquire real estate at tremendous discounts, and terrific cash flows.

Notes:

Ideas on utilizing discounted mortgages with substitution of collateral

1. NEGOTIATE A LOWER RATE THAN THE RATE ON THE NOTES

The notes being used as collateral (notes bought at a discount) could have a higher interest rate than the rate you are able to negotiate with the seller of the property you are acquiring.

2. INCREASE THE YIELD ON THE NOTE BEING SUBSTITUTED PRIOR TO SUBSTITUTION

If the note you are going to use to substitute as collateral can be restructured to increase the yield, then you can replace the note with another note that is comparable to the one you just improved.

3. EARLY PAYOFF AND SUBSTITUTE

For example, if the note you have used as collateral has a face value of $10,000, which you bought for $6,000, you would still owe $10,000. However, you could negotiate with the payer to pay it off at a discount. If the note is paid off for say $9,000, then take $6,000 and buy another $10,000 note to substitute for collateral. This leaves you $3000, which is your profit.

4. FORECLOSE

If the note goes into default, and you are well secured, you could foreclose and acquire a substantial equity. Could you not then create a new note against the property you just acquired in foreclosure and use any of the endless techniques you have learned?

5. CASH FLOW FROM DIFFERENT RATES

If there is a difference in the interest rates between the notes being used as collateral and your note to the seller, depending on how the notes are structured, the seller's note could pay off early or you could have a positive cash flow coming to you each month.

Notes:

Increasing the yield - increasing the profit

Another way to increase your profit is to increase your yield. For example, if your yield on a note is based on a payment of $150 per month and the payment was increased to $300 per month, your yield would increase tremendously. It would be a win-win situation, providing a benefit for both the payer and the payee.

The power of partials –

Buying the partial to increase the yield

Suppose you have an individual who has a mortgage that they took back on a house that they had been trying to sell forever. They really didn't want to take a mortgage back, but it was necessary in order to sell the house. The mortgage has a principal face amount of $20,000. The interest rate is 8% per annum, amortized over 10 years (120 mos.). The payment is $242.66 per month. They need some cash (around $5,000), but they don't want to take a deep discount like all the other buyers of notes have offered them. Is there a way to make this a win-win situation? The answer is a resounding YES! Suppose you offer to buy one fourth of the mortgage ($5,000) for $5,000. Is this a typographical error? No. Offer to buy the next 30 payments of $242.66 per month for $5000. The remaining payments at the end of 30 months are reassigned to the seller. Did the seller get exactly what they were asking? YES. Was there a discount? No. Put the figures into the calculator and determine the yield.

YIELD= _____

This is the stuff of which fortunes are created. Suppose further that you don't have the $5000 to pay them. How will you get it and still make an enormous yield? If you have been asleep so far in the course. WAKE UP NOW!

Notes:

Boy! Did I buy the farm with this one (literally)

How to buy a business with no money down using discounted notes

The American dream is to own your own business. But it takes money to buy a business. Right? But not necessarily your own money. Many would be entrepreneurs have been led to believe that they have to go through the pain and humiliation of crawling on their knees to a bank, or worse to the SBA where they want a mortgage on your first born and all of your grand-children. Is there a better way? Yes, Virginia, there is a Santa Claus, and No, Dorothy we no longer have to deal with the Kansas National Bank anymore. Most businesses are sold with some owner financing that comes with it. Each deal is different, but you can do a pretty good job structuring a business buyout utilizing discounted notes. Let me give you a real life example.

There was a business in Northern Florida. It had a good cash flow, and the owner was willing to do some owner financing. The banks would not touch the deal mainly because they did not understand the business (do they ever?). The SBA would do it if the buyer was willing to mortgage everything he owned, his wife owned, personal guarantees by him, his wife, his relatives, etc., etc., You get the picture. Here are the numbers: The purchase price was $230,000. The real estate appraised for far more than that. The seller was willing to take $180,000 cash at closing and a second note and mortgage for $50,000. A first note and mortgage was created and sold simultaneously at closing. The terms were: $230.000 principal, 10% interest rate, amortized over a 180 month period (15 years) with payments of $2,471.59. The second mortgage was for $50,000 principal, 10% interest amortized over 180 months with no prepayment penalty. . Payments were $537.30 per month. The business paid all the notes and expenses plus a nice profit each year.

Here is the nice part. The first note was sold at closing simultaneously with the purchase of the business. The institutional investor that bought the note and mortgage required a 11.5% yield. After discounting this unseasoned note ($230,000 - 10% int. 180 mos) to a 11.5% yield, the institutional buyer of the note paid $211,574.50. The buyer of the business paid the seller of the business $180, 000 cash and gave a second note for $50,000 to the seller. WAIT A MIN-UTE! There must be an arithmetic error! There is $31,574.50 left over. Ummm. You are right. I guess that goes into HIP National Bank. Do you see the POWER of discounted notes and mortgages now?

Notes:

The Power of Simultaneous Closings

An Interview With Robert Leonetti & Jayme Kahla of Success Investments

Success Investments, a leader in the field of purchasing seller-financed transactions, was founded in 1994 by partners Jayme Kahla and Robert Leonetti. Jayme's initial interest in the note business stemmed from her background as a CPA and real estate syndicator; Bob's from his years as a creative finance instructor and mortgage lender. The combined experience of the principals of the company exceeds 30 years in the real estate and mortgage brokerage fields. It is their goal to become one of the top 10 buyers of secondary mortgages throughout the United States. In addition, they hope to expand into Canada within the next year and provide a funding source for real estate not presently available.

What is a simultaneous closing?

Jayme: A simultaneous closing is where there is a transfer or sale of property, and a note created between the buyer and seller is purchased by an investor at the same closing table where the real estate transaction is taking place.

Why is it important for brokers and investors to learn about simultaneous closings?

Jayme: With all the people coming out of seminars, most of the existing notes are difficult to find. In order to cut down on the problems of competition we started to focus more on buying paper right at the settlement table. When you are working with this type of paper you are working with a note you know is marketable.

Bob: It's also a great service to the marketplace. Because of my background as a mortgage broker, I know all the programs that are available to home buyers. When I first got into the note business and discovered simultaneous closings, I realized that this meets a huge need. Once Realtors discover that this is another tool they can put in their toolbox, they are very excited.

What is the advantage to the note broker?

The great advantage to the note broker is that there is no one else bidding on the paper.

There is also an opportunity for a good profit nine times out of ten, when the note broker goes to a property seller and asks him what his cash needs are, they are going to get a number. The most common response is, "I want all of my money." After speaking with them, the broker can generally get a specific number. The seller may need to payoff an underlying lien, pay transaction commissions, or get enough for a down payment on a new home. By talking with the seller and finding out exactly what he needs, we can see if we need to do, for example a partial purchase, where we can buy part of the paper and pass through some payments back to the seller, or part of a balloon, or part of each payment. There are many ways to structure the deals. But the main thing is finding out what the seller needs.

Bob: Simultaneous closings also make it easier to find paper. If you're targeting private note holders via direct mail or advertising, you're expending a lot of effort and money just to get that one person in the door. Whereas when you use simultaneous closings and talk with a group of 15 Realtors, each one of those Realtors may have one, two or three scenarios where this might work for their borrowers or sellers. The same thing applies when you talk with mortgage brokers.

It's a matter of leveraging your time and marketing investments. Instead of trying to find and buy the existing notes, you buy them before they hit the market.

Specifically, how would a broker go about putting together a simultaneous closing?

Bob: We have found that there are three major areas in which to work. The first is FSBO (For Sale By Owner) property. Contact the owner and say something like, "Not every single buyer that comes along will qualify for a conventional loan. Why not sell your home a little quicker by doing some creative advertising, such as '10% Down, Owner Will Carry, Easy Qualifying." We find that when people put that ad in the papers, they are getting a tremendous response.

The second area is Realtors. You are offering them a solution to sell more properties in a quicker amount of time. If they have a buyer who doesn't qualify for a conventional loan, rather than turn away the deal, you can help them figure out a way to do the deal.

Mortgage brokers are the third area. Make it clear to them that you are not competing with mortgage brokers. You are offering a service and a way to close deals that is outside the normal realm of mortgage brokers.

Doesn't, the note seller see what the note broker makes at the simultaneous closing settlement table?

Jayme: No. At the sale of the property there has to be a HUD closing statement The sale of the note does not appear on that statement, it is strictly the sale of the property. What does show up is that the seller is carrying back the full amount of the note. That is all that is required.

Suppose a broker cultivates referral sources, such as Realtors and mortgage brokers that can send him notes on a regular basis, whether through simultaneous closings or the more traditional method. Once the investor discovers the broker's sources, what prevents him from dealing directly with them in the future to get notes and cutting the broker out of the loop?

Bob: Obviously we can't speak for any other investors, but we have a very strong policy that our brokers are our personal clients. We cannot afford to go behind their backs and cut them out.

Jayme has a broker/client right now, a cotton farmer in Lubbock, Texas, who calls us from his tractor when he's out in the field. Jayme, how long has Bryan been with us?

Jayme; About 5 years. What happened is that Bryan found a seller with a large number of notes. After Bryan brokered the first couple of notes to us, the seller, Tommy, contacted us to sell the rest. He said he figured he could get more money if he dealt directly with us. I told him that was not the case. We would not pay him any more than he would get through his broker. Now he does deal directly with us, but any time we close a deal with him, we pay Brian also, even though he was not involved.

What are the major selling points a broker should make to his referral sources to convince them that simultaneous closings are the way to go?

Bob: First, remind them that traditional lending underwriting has a great number of requirements that simultaneous closing underwriters don't look at. For example, if someone applies for a loan, Fannie Mae ratios require that their house payment plus their revolving monthly debt payment does not exceed 38% of their gross monthly income. Simultaneous closing underwriters do not have that criteria. Additionally, traditional underwriters want to know where the down payment funds are coming from. Simultaneous closing underwriters don't care. Traditional underwriters require that the applicant has been in the same job for at least the last two years. if he has been self-employed for less than a couple of years, they are hesitant about approving the loan. Simultaneous closing underwriters don't have that criteria.

- 113 -

In addition, the buyer will save tremendously in closing costs. The average closing costs on a $100,000 house purchase using a conventional loan are about $4,000. The same transaction using seller financing in a simultaneous closing costs about $900.

Notes:

_____

_____

_____

_____

_____

_____

_____

_____

_____

_____

_____

Simultaneous closings: A creative alternative financing device or an originated loan?

Steps to Avoid the Later.

By Michael Morrongiello

In recent years I have seen the proliferation of simultaneous closings used by many note brokers as a means of generating quality paper that can be bought and/or brokered to investors eager to get funds out. In fact, one major institution claims that almost 40% of their monthly production is newly created paper that is generated by the use of this technique. This creative financing alternative can assist motivated sellers in moving their properties quickly or help buyers who otherwise might not be able to obtain traditional financing, get into a home.

If properly set up, assisting parties that need our help can be rewarding. However, this burgeoning facet of the discounted note industry can be fraught with dangerous risk if improperly used. Whenever a technique that makes it easier to obtain credit for consumers becomes popular, and more acceptable to use, it invites those individuals with questionable motives to participate. Fraudulent down payments, over inflated property sale prices, questionable contracts, fabricated or "doctored" documents, etc., are just a few of the areas of abuse that have surfaced when dealing with newly created paper.

Note brokers and investors today, who deal in purchasing newly created notes, need to be very careful about making sure they are not crossing the line into the highly regulated world of loan originations. To have a deal they put together characterized as a loan origination will not bode well for them or the note industry. It is imperative that both investors and brokers take certain steps to thwart any potential issues, which might characterize a simultaneous closing as a loan instead of a simple, non-RESPA, secondary market assignment of a security instrument.

I have reviewed some of the allegations in a recent lawsuit, about a property that was to be sold for $43,000 cash. Then, because the buyer could not obtain traditional financing, the sales price was magically inflated to $59,900 so the sellers could take back a $54,000 note which was when discounted to produce roughly the initial cash sales amount. This scenario is one that has the potential to be abused over and over again in the marketplace. Realtors, mortgage brokers. and property sellers themselves tend to inflate the sales price of properties as a means of compensating for the "discount" they will have to take when selling the purchase money note for immediate cash. This should never be done. Using this technique is an invitation for a lawsuit from a disgruntled buyer who feels that they were taken advantage of.

In today's litigious society, anyone can file a lawsuit with phony allegations. However, there are some steps brokers and investors can take to distance themselves from having a simultaneous closing transaction construed as a loan origination. It should be noted that the following points illustrated are meant to spur careful consideration and thought among you. I am not in the business of rendering legal or professional advice, which should be sought for further protective strategies.

(1) Advertise and sell a property for its full, retail, fair market value. Never attempt to oversell the property's price simply because you are providing financing terms. You never see furniture, appliance, or audio electronic retailers inflate sales prices even though they offer financing incentives like no interest for one year, etc. That they sell their goods and services for full retail markup and then because they are able to then factor their financing receivables for cash liquidity or simply hold on to it for the interest income it produces.

(2) Use generic credit applications to establish an employment and income profile of the potential buyer/payers of property. Insistence on using the industry standard "FNMA 1003 Uniform Residential Loan Application", potentially creates ties too closely associated with the loan origination business.

(3) Have credit authorizations forms made out in favor of the property seller and/or their assigns instead of to you or your lender. What must be clear to the parties involved is that the seller is the one that is extending the financing, not the note broker or note investor.

(4) Never contractually agree to purchase a note before it is created. It is one thing to use illustrative scenarios such as "suppose this" and "what if that. However, entering into a formal contract to purchase a note before it has been created is dangerous.

(5) Make certain that any closing settlement statements or HUD--I 's, etc., do not list you, the note broker, or the note investor, as the "lender". In the space provided, make certain the described lender is the seller of the property.

(6) If possible, refrain from dealing with buyers. Let the seller or the seller's realtor interface with them and fine-tune the actual terms of the sale, down payment, and acceptable repayment terms for the purchase money mortgage and note.

(7) Wait until the mortgage and note documents have been executed and some time has elapsed before funding. The amount of time is up to you and your perception of the issues of risk. It could be several hours, the next day, or after the first installment has been paid by the new debtors.

(8) Think carefully whether or not you want to require that Federal Truth In Lending disclosure forms be provided to the buyer by the seller, or closing agent, as part of the closing documentation. There are two (2) schools of thought to carefully consider; A) Having these disclosures required, acknowledged, and executed by the buyer, creates the appearance that the financing offered is more like traditional financing other lenders use where this requirement is the norm. B) Not requiring such a document supports the argument that this financing is a private seller financed transaction, exempt from such disclosures. The exception to this thinking is where a seller regularly offers to finance properties. Such sellers, in effect, are considered "dealers" or financiers of real estate and as such, may be required to provide such disclosures. And, in some states like California, they must be licensed.

(9) Use a disclaimer statement, acknowledged and executed by both buyers and sellers, whereby they agree that the financing and disclosures provided are private financing not necessarily tied to any Federal or State requirements.

(10) Insist on adding the verbiage "this is a purchase money mortgage" to the security instrument executed. There are certain implicit protections that go along with the inclusion of this language. Consult with your attorney for more details.

It is my observation that investors urging the use of standard loan origination documentation as part of their processing packaging, verifying and due diligence procedures are treading on a very blurred line. In an attempt to make the simultaneous closing of a private seller financed transaction more consistent with loans that were originated, they are in actuality beckoning further scrutiny. The cliché "if it looks like a duck..." shouldn't be taken lightly here. There is no need to make a seller financed deal look like a loan origination and to do so invites comparison.

Notes:

Negotiations

Now that you know some basic concepts of seller carry-back financing, let's discuss the negotiations involved. Begin by looking at the elements of a real estate transaction

- Price
- Terms
- Interest rates
- Cash payments
- Closing costs (who pays)
- Impound accounts
- Title company to use
- Escrow company to use
- Release of loan liability for seller
- Personal property included or not
- Time of possession
- Repairs or deferred maintenance
- Appraisal

Seller Carry-back Financing

What do all of the above elements have in common? They are NEGOTIABLE. Some people act as if they don't understand its meaning. Few transactions have as many negotiable elements as a real estate transaction. You will have far more difficulty negotiating loan terms and conditions with the Bank than with a Seller who is carrying back a trust deed note or mortgage to facilitate the sale of his /her property.

If you remember nothing else from this course, remember that all real estate transactions are negotiable. It is sometimes difficult to be objective about your own situation.

Negotiating Terms on A Seller Carry-back Note

Although all note amounts and terms are negotiable, the first items most commonly negotiated between buyer and seller on a note are:

- Amount of the note (how much of the purchase price the seller will carry-back)

- Interest rate

- Monthly payment

- Due date (or balloon payment, if any)

Notes:

_____

_____

_____

_____

_____

_____

_____

_____

_____

_____

Items to consider when drawing a note

INTEREST RATE: (typically written as an annual rate although the payment is paid monthly) A vital element in the note. What the seller receives as a rate of return must be clearly spelled out.

AMOUNT OF THE PAYMENT TO BE MADE IN EACH PERIOD. This figure should be specific to avoid misunderstanding.

ATTORNEYS' FEE CLAUSE: A buyer/payer might like to avoid this, but it is a necessity for the seller/payee. If a payer doesn't pay or a misunderstanding arises and ruins everyone's day, it is best NOT to be on the paying end of attorney fees. Their hourly rates continue to rise with inflation and can mount up quickly. Knowing which items should be in a note is important, but only a beginning. Whoever draws the note must be aware of other issues:

USURY: Usury means charging a rate of interest on a loan that exceeds the interest rate limit imposed by state law.

IMPUTED INTEREST: The opposite of usury (charging too much interest) is charging too little interest. From a legal standpoint it is OK not to charge any interest! However, from an income tax standpoint, if a certain minimum interest rate is not charged, the IRS will IMPUTE (put in place) a certain rate of interest. Imputed interest rate rules fall under Internal Revenue Code Section 483 and § 1271 through § 1274. The Internal Revenue Service has a formula to determine what that rate will be at any time. If you plan to carry a note at less than 9% interest, see your accountant or attorney for the current imputed interest rate formula.

Read the next paragraph only if you are technically curious. Otherwise, skip it. Imputed interest rate calculations present a classic example of bureaucracy:

If seller financing is $2.8 Million or less the interest rate on that financing must be at least 9% or the relevant Applicable Federal Rate (AFR, whichever is lower. The relevant Applicable Federal Rate is below 9% today. (In mid 1998), but it fluctuates. The relevant Applicable Federal Rate is the lower of: I) those rates in effect in the month the sales contract is written (not closed) or, 2) the rates in effect in the prior two months. Each month IRS issues a set of Applicable Federal Interest Rates. The IRS bases the rates on yields of Treasury securities with roughly comparable terms to maturity. The short term Applicable Rate is for seller financing that lasts up to 3 years. The median Applicable Rate is based on the yields for Treasury securities with terms of more than three years, up to and including 9 years. The long-term Applicable Rate is for financing maturities of 10 years or more. Within those classifications are four others, based on how often the payments of principal and interest are to be made on the note: monthly, quarterly, semiannually or annually. These rates also set a floor for interest the seller may charge a buyer of real estate without the IRS imputing the higher rate of interest. As we said, a study in bureaucracy!

Notes:

_____

_____

_____

_____

_____

_____

_____

_____

_____

_____

Variable or adjustable interest rates on carry-back notes:

Some sellers would like to copy lending institutions by carrying a secured note that has a variable rate of interest (one that is adjusted periodically). BE CAREFUL. Federal regulations have an impact. In some states usury may be an issue. DO NOT attempt to set up an adjustable rate carry-back note without a VERY GOOD REAL ESTATE ATTORNEY.

LATE CHARGES: Example of a late charge clause in a note:

IN THE EVENT ANY PAYMENT IS NOT PAID WITHIN 10 DAYS OF THE DUE DATE, MORTGAGOR SHALL PAY TO MORTGAGEE A LATE CHARGE OF SIX PER CENT (6%) OF THE PAYMENT DUE.

A late charge provision is a penalty clause inserted in a note to discourage the payer from being late. Most institutional and private investors who hold notes secured by real estate allow a grace period (usually 10 to 15 days) before the late charge is applied.

PREPAYMENT PENALTY: If a seller does not want his loan paid in full before the due date, the seller may put wording in the note that the buyer must pay several months of interest in addition to the principal due in order to pay off the note. Such wording is called a prepayment penalty.

For the seller a prepayment penalty is an exception to the "MORE SOONER IS BETTER" rule. The reason: Suppose a property seller is in a low tax bracket. He structures the note payments so that the gain on the sale is spread over a period of years where much or all of the gain is taxed in a lower tax bracket. An early payoff could accelerate the remaining gain and push the seller into a higher tax bracket. If that were to happen, then the "MORE SOONER IS BETTER" rule may not be good for that seller. A prepayment penalty may be good for a lender but is not good for a borrower. A note does not permit prepayment when the words "or more" are omitted from the note in describing the periodic payment amount.

DUE-ON-SALE: This clause gives the mortgagee the right but not the obligation to accelerate the note's due date when a buyer sells his property. Most notes use an "alienation clause" as the due-on-sale clause. When the borrower alienates title (transfers title to another), an alienation clause gives the mortgagee the right to accelerate the note balance, which is then immediately payable. The note holder need not accelerate but may negotiate some new terms on the note. A "due-an-sale" clause is the common reference for this. Here is some sample wording.

"If the mortgagor shall sell, convey or alienate said property, or any part thereof, or any interest therein, or shall be divested of his title in any manner or way, whether voluntarily or involuntarily, without the written consent of the mortgagee being first notified and approval obtained, mortgagee shall have the right, at its option, to declare any indebtedness or obligations secured hereby, irrespective of the maturity date specified in any note evidencing the same, immediately due and payable."

Interest rate, size and frequency of payments, late charges, prepayment penalties, due-on-sale clauses all are negotiable between a willing buyer and a willing seller, within statutory limits imposed by the state.

Notes:

_____

_____

_____

_____

_____

_____

_____

_____

Seven secrets of successful negotiators

By John Schaub

Do you consider yourself a good negotiator?

When I decided to teach a new seminar on negotiation, I began studying every book on negotiation I could find. I consider myself an excellent negotiator, and yet I learned many ways to improve.

Whether negotiating for the purchase of the Empire State Building or the release of hostages, professional negotiators seemed to agree on several strategies.

Great negotiators learn their craft from others. Negotiating, like many things in life, is a skill you can continue to improve. Like management, negotiating is more complex than it first appears. It is not simply a matter of haggling over the price, as you would when buying a melon at a roadside stand. Likewise, the best negotiator is not the flashy, smooth talker. The best negotiator is the one who is best prepared. Negotiating is a learnable craft, and one that you should set a goal to learn. It pays better than any other skill you can acquire.

Secret #1 — Avoid Emotional Involvement

First, admit that emotions can play a big part in your decision-making process. When you are angry or scared, you make decisions differently than when you are happy and secure. When negotiating with sellers, buyers, note payers and tenants, you can become emotional. Imagine how you would react if just before closing a note, a seller told you he wasn't going to go through with the sale until you threw in a brand new Mercedes?

You cannot prevent yourself from feeling your emotions, but you can recognize that you are angry or upset, and refuse to negotiate further until you are in full control again. You can even begin to anticipate situations that may evoke an emotional reaction on your part and prepare for it ahead of time.

Secret #2 — Research Before You Begin

When buying or selling notes, you should research the property, paperwork, the market, and the people involved. If you are buying, then check out the sellers to learn all you can about their situation. The first step is to ask them a lot of questions. You can learn a lot in this informal stage of negotiation. Once you begin making offers, the sellers will be on their guard and reveal little about their situation. When I teach my Making It Big On Little Deals seminar, students, armed with a long list of questions, call property sellers and get them to reveal much more than they should about their personal situation and the property.

You should know if the seller must sell, if they have any real or perceived deadlines, and as much as can you learn about their financial situation. This gives you information that will help you craft an offer they can accept, and assures you an acceptable profit.

Know everything you can about the note and property, especially their real market values. Know your market conditions. Is this a situation where you will have a lot of competition, or will you be the only one making an offer? At what price can you resell this note quickly? The market conditions dictate how quickly you make your offer and how much you offer.

Secret #3 – Have A Game Plan

Whenever possible, negotiate on your terms and at a time and place that you choose. When you are the buyer, you can generally direct how negotiations will proceed. No one can force you to make an offer, although the seller may pressure you by revealing that another offer is coming. I suggest that you don't compete with this other offer. Simply say, "Call me if the other offer doesn't materialize" (which often happens).

Based on all of the information you have gathered, calculate the highest price you are willing to pay, the lowest price that you can imagine the sellers accepting, and do this for both a full purchase and a partial purchase. Write down the terms that are important to you. Know what you are willing to give away and what you will insist on to make the deal.

Write all of this down, and then formulate your offer, asking for your best deal. Be prepared to make counteroffers without giving away what is important to you. Sellers ("agents") will work hard trying to get you to pay more. They may appeal to your sense of fairness, greed, or whatever they can work on. It is important to have a written game plan before you enter into the excitement of the negotiation.

Secret #4 – Be Aware Of Your Power And Use It Wisely

You will often have more power than the other party when negotiating. As a buyer, you always have more power. You never have to buy and they often have to sell. That is why you lock in your profits when you buy. When you sell, the buyer has the power.

It is possible to overpower or over-leverage a situation. Imagine the seller facing bankruptcy. They have been chased by creditors and possibly harassed by other note buyers. These sellers are close to just throwing in the towel and refusing to negotiate with anyone.

If you make them a take-it-or-leave-it offer, they will probably leave it. To buy a note in this situation, you must make an offer that shows them that you care about what happens to them. At this end of the negotiations, both parties should still have some honor intact. If you take it all, you run the very real risk that the other party will refuse to perform as agreed. Write down the best you expect and the worst you are able to accept before you start, and you won't be misled into negotiating for more than you should.

Secret #5 — Put Yourself In Their Shoes

If you were declaring bankruptcy or losing your house in foreclosure, how would you feel? Would you be worried about where to move, about what your family and friends think about your financial management skills, and about being able to buy a house or get credit again?

By letting the seller know that you can identify with these fears, and that you are willing to try to solve some of their problems, you will have a better chance of buying the note. These sellers often postpone making any decision until the very last minute. I am negotiating to buy two houses today from two different sellers that will be sold this week at a foreclosure sale. The sellers have had months to do something, but have taken no action. A psychologist might say they are in denial.

Secret #6 — Know What Risk You Are Taking And Have An Alternative

Whatever you are negotiating for, there is a downside risk that you will not prevail. Usually the risk is small. Children are typically fearless negotiators because they know that perhaps the worst that will happen is that they will be confined to their room for some time and to reflect. If you are negotiating to buy a note and you don't get it, you haven't really lost the profit you were going to make; you have just postponed it until you find the next deal. It's not your last chance to buy a note.

Try to always have at least two potential deals to consider. If the first seller becomes intractable, shift your efforts to the other note and make them an offer you like better. Perhaps the first seller will come around when he realizes there is real competition for your money.

Identify the worst that can happen: you don't buy, so you keep your money for another month; or if you're a real estate investor, you don't rent, so the house sits empty for a few more weeks; or you don't sell the house and you have to make another month's payment. All of these are better than paying too much when you buy, renting to the wrong tenant, or selling a note or a house or anything else too cheaply.

Secret #7 — Know When to Close the Deal

A good salesman knows when to stop talking and start writing. A good negotiator knows when the deal is good enough and stops negotiating. You can negotiate for more than you should, causing the other party to withdraw or even to renege on a previously agreed deal, even if you have a signed contract!

You can also simply talk too much. Once you reached your goals and the deal is good enough, stop talking and write down your agreement. When you are buying a note, write down every point you want to negotiate before you start, and note each point of agreement as you go. At the end, you can simply draft a formal contract based on what you have already resolved.

Legal Matters

The question that often arises among note buyers is whether you should ever accept a copy of a note from the seller. The answer to that question is a resounding no. Legally, the reason is very simple. You want to buy a negotiable instrument. You must also want to be the legal holder of that note. In order to be the legal holder, the original note must be in your possession and it must be properly endorsed to you. It is certainly alright to have a copy of the note in your initial negotiations with the seller, but always insure that he has the original note. Never show up at a closing and without the original note being in the seller's possession.

There are several reasons why you want to be the legal holder of the note. First, you want to be sure that someone else doesn't possess the note. If you accept a copy of the note, then the seller could possibly sell the note to another individual and there would be no way that you would get your money back.

Second, sometime in the future, you may want to resell the note or borrow money against it. A financial institution or another lender will never lend money against a copy of the note. In fact, they will insist upon possession of the note at the time they lend you money or at the time you sell the note to the buyer.

Third, you want the right to receive the payments from the payer. Legally, the payer would not have to make payments to you in the event that you did not hold the original note.

Fourth, you want to be sure of what you're buying. Also, at the time you receive possession of the original note, compare it with any copies that you may have been working with during your negotiations. The working copy must be an exact duplicate of the original.

Some individuals feel that an Affidavit of Lost Note signed by the seller would be sufficient in the event that you could not produce the original note. However, such an affidavit cannot take the place of the original note. It does not make you a holder.

Also, title insurance companies will not protect you either. Title insurance insures that the lien against the real estate is valid. It does not insure ownership of the note.

What can you do in the event that the seller cannot find the note? The best solution is to have the payer sign a new original note. Good luck in getting this done, however, as the payer has no obligation to sign a new note and will often refuse to do so.

Also, at closing it is absolutely necessary that you have the note endorsed to you. Even though you have possession of the original note, if it is not properly endorsed, you are not a holder of the note.

Notes:

_____

_____

_____

_____

_____

_____

_____

_____

_____

What is a proper endorsement?

Where should the endorsement appear? Generally, the endorsement appears on the back of the note, similar to in the way you endorse the back of a check. However, an endorsement may be written on a separate piece of paper and if it is permanently attached to the original note, it becomes part of the note. In the law, this is called an Allonge.

An endorsement is not a very complex item. The simplest, nonqualified endorsement says, "PAY TO THE ORDER OF: (YOUR NAME)" and signed and dated by the seller. It is very important to note that if the seller does not wish any further liability on the note, a typical qualified endorsement would say, "PAY TO THE ORDER OF: (YOUR NAME) WITHOUT RECOURSE" and it is signed by the seller and dated.

Recourse defined

Georgia law provides that if the endorsement makes no mention either way about recourse, then the note is endorsed "with recourse".

This question of endorsement is greatly misunderstood in the note industry. It is important to understand what "recourse" and "without recourse" means because recourse can be one of the most important features of a note negotiation.

A note sold with "recourse" makes the seller liable to pay you if the payments are not made. This is called a "nonqualified" endorsement. A note sold "without recourse" means that the seller does not have to pay you if payment stops. This is called a "qualified" endorsement. If the endorsement makes no mention either way about recourse, Georgia law says that the note is endorsed "with recourse". This silence feature can be a trap for the unknowing.

A number of note sellers will object to endorsing "with recourse". They are selling the note at a discount and want to be out of the picture. They feel that it is unfair to suffer the discount and still have to guarantee the note.

Most note buyers, on the other hand, prefer endorsement "with recourse" for the simple reason that it provides one more possible source from which to obtain payment on a note. Note buyers may also become suspicious of the quality of the note if the seller is not willing to endorse "with recourse".

Many times, the subject of recourse or non-recourse is not discussed at all because neither party is aware that recourse is in fact an issue. Sellers rarely ask about recourse, because they don't know that they should. Note buyers are more likely to be aware of recourse, although many of them are not, and may obtain an endorsement that is silent on the issue, not being aware that the seller is liable to pay. On the other hand, some eager note buyers may take advantage of the ignorance of the unknowing seller, and deliberately fail to discuss recourse, and then obtain an endorsement that silently obligates the seller to pay.

To avoid any later litigation, I would suggest that you do not use silent endorsement. The endorsement should say: "For Value Received, Paid to the Order of (your name) with (or without) Recourse" so that it is clearly stated in writing.

There is an additional problem that may arise if you buy a note endorsed "with recourse" that you should be aware . If it is necessary later on to enforce your recourse rights against the seller, which will probably require court action, the seller may sue you for usury. Usury is charging an illegally high interest rate. Even though the interest rate on the note may be legal, when combined with the discount in which you bought it, your total yield may push you over the legal limit and subject you to very severe penalties. The potential consequences vary greatly from state to state.

Seller's usury claims are only a concern when your endorsement is "with recourse". The problem does not exist in endorsements "without recourse".

The Six Possible Player Payers

It is interesting to note that there are six possible people obligated to pay the note, in addition to the person making the payments.

(1) THE MAKER

The maker is the person who signed the original note and is responsible to make payments. In most situations, it is the maker who is the person making the payments.

In some instances, the maker is no longer making payments because he has sold the property. Even though someone else is making the payments, the maker continues to have legal responsibility until the note is paid off. If there are more than one makers on the note, each is responsible to pay the entire note. The payers are commonly called co-makers or co-signers. When a husband and wife sign a note as co-makers they're both equally obligated on the note. In the event of a divorce later, they're probably both still obligated to pay the note even though the divorce decree may provide that one party is responsible for the debt.

(2) ASSUMPTION OF NOTE.

If the property has been sold without paying off the note, the new owner may have assumed the payers note debt. "Assuming the debt," means that the new owner accepts legal responsibility for making the payments on the note. Even if the maker is no longer making the payments, the maker's liability for the payment remains.

The property may have been sold several times, with each succeeding owner assuming the note. In these cases, each person, who at one time assumed the note, continues to be responsible and is a possible payer. Many times, the maker and other former owners of the property are not aware of their continuing liability on the note.

(3) "SUBJECT TO"

A person may purchase the property without assuming the note debt. This type of new owner is commonly said to have purchased the property "subject to" the existing debt. Even though this new owner is making payments, there is no personal liability because no assumption took place. The new owner still is a possible payer however, because the incentive to avoid losing the property by keeping the payments current.

(4) GUARANTOR

The guarantor is the person who promises to pay the note if there is a default. When the maker doesn't pay the note, the guarantor is responsible to pay. Some common guarantors are friends, parents, or relatives to ensure payments on behalf of a maker who lacks financial strength or suffers from a poor credit rating.

It must be noted that individuals involved in a corporation with limited assets, may sign personally to ensure payment on a note on property sold belonging to a corporation. Guarantors are possible payers, but they are only liable if the maker of the note does not pay.

(5) ENDORSER WITH RECOURSE.

Another possible payer may be a seller who sold or assigned rights to collect the payments on the note. When the note is sold or assigned, it is endorsed on the back like a check. If the person selling you the note is not the person who originally sold the property, chances are the note has been endorsed. In most cases, the endorsement of a note means that the seller of the note guarantees the payment will be made. This guarantee is referred to as "with recourse" which means that any subsequent owner of the note can seek payment from the endorser if the note is not paid. Any endorser of a note is a possible payer. However, if the seller endorsed "without recourse" on the back of the note at the time of the endorsement, then the note seller did not guarantee payment and is not legally responsible to pay.

(6) JUNIOR LIEN HOLDERS

After the property has been purchased, it may be used by the owner or creditors of the owners, as a pledge to ensure other debts and obligations are being paid.

These other holders of other debts and obligations, which attach to the property, are referred to as, "junior lien holders."

Typical junior lien holders are second and third mortgage lenders, judgment creditors, state or internal revenue service tax liens, or mechanics liens. These liens holders have a lower priority than the security for your note and usually do not impair your security.

These junior lien holders may be possible payers. Even though they are not legally obligated to pay your note, as a practical matter, they may do so. If there is a default, junior lien holders may choose to protect their inferior claim to the property by making payments on your notes. If they fail to do so, the junior lien holds may be extinguished in a foreclosure.

Silent seconds

There is a growing market in the second mortgage business as more and more sellers are taking a second mortgage as part of the sales price in real estate transactions. This can be a lucrative business if you are very careful.

If it looks too good to be true, it may actually be hidden from the first mortgage lender as a "silent second." Silent seconds are not acceptable risks. They are usually kept silent because the buyer cannot qualify for a large enough loan from the first mortgage lender and the seller, anxious to close the deal, secretly accepts the second mortgage to make up the difference in what is know as a "silent second." Many note buyers and sellers innocently enter into these silent second transactions not realizing that this practice is illegal. This practice is so wide spread that FNMA (Fannie Mae) coined the term "silent seconds" to alert the financial community of the problem.

Fraudulent financing

The first mortgage lender may be unaware that the buyer did not pay the full down payment and that the buyer signed a second secured note to the seller. If the first mortgage lender knew about the note, they would not have approved the first loan because the buyer may not have had enough income to qualify. Many lenders have policies that specifically state that no secondary financing is allowed.

In order to protect yourself, always ask for copies of notes and recorded mortgage documents, the recorded deed from the seller to the buyer (the warranty deed), and the closing statement. If the face amount of the note isn't shown on the closing statement somewhere, it's almost certainly a silent second. If the recorded second mortgage was not recorded within a few days of the vesting deed and the first mortgage, you probably have a silent second.

Always do your due diligence. Call the first mortgage lender. Ask if they are aware that a second mortgage exists. Do not imply or state that anything is wrong with the second mortgage; you are simply trying to find out. Mail or fax the first mortgage lender a copy of the note and mortgage that you have been offered. Make sure that they are aware that the note exists. This is certainly a problem you want to avoid. To be safe, don't buy silent seconds.

The Usury Trap

Charging excess interest rates is called usury. There are laws to protect people from paying too much interest. People who buy seller financed notes are normally not concerned about usury because usury laws rarely apply to these transactions. There are situations, however, in which usury can become a problem and you, as the note buyer should be aware of them to avoid financially devastating penalties. In most seller-financed transactions, the interest rate of a note is not usurious. Here it is perfectly legal. Such a note results from the sale of real estate. The seller sells the real estate to another person who pays the cash down payment and signs a monthly payment note to the seller agreeing to pay a rate of interest that is legal for that state. The person who bought the property and signed the note is the payer. Later, the seller decided to sell the note for cash and offers it to you, the note buyer, for less than what the payer owes. This is a discount. The discount may be as large as you and the seller agree because usury laws do not ordinarily apply to discounts granted by the seller. With a discount granted by the seller, you can increase your total yield to, lets say 20%. This total yield may be above state usury limits, but the payer is still only paying the stated interest rate on the note. Nothing changes for the payer and the stated interest rate is not illegal.

Pitfall Problems With Usury

The most obvious pitfall is the note that was made with an illegally high interest rate on it, usually because the seller and payer are unaware of the usury limits. The seller has unintentionally broken the usury law but is never the less subject to the penalties that can be claimed by the payer. It is incumbent upon you as a purchaser of a seller financed note to check the usury statutes of the state where the note was originated.

Selling The Real Estate And The Note Simultaneously

The second potential pitfall with usury arises when the seller sells the real estate and the note at the same time. This usually occurs when the seller was unwilling to carry a note in the first place and is merely using the note as a way to get all cash from the sale of the real estate. This is commonly referred to in the notes industry as a "simultaneous closing," or a "point of purchase closing," or "table funding."

In this situation, two questions arise. First, who is the real lender-you or the seller? Are you buying a non-usurious note from the seller at a discount, or are you a lender originating a usurious 20% loan to the buyer? Second, is the buyer directly or indirectly reimbursing the seller for the discount? If the buyer is paying more than the property is worth or makes a side deal to reimburse the seller for the discount, this may be considered interest charged to the payer and may be illegal. This is an unclear area in the usury law. One way to avoid this problem is to buy notes that have seasoning of at least two or three months or more.

Amending the note

The third problem arises from trying to maintain your yield by changing the terms of the note if the payer cannot meet some obligation. The typical example is a non-usurious note that was all due at the end of a three year period. To purchase the note at a discount to yield 15%, the payer asks you for an extension at the end of the three years because he does not have the money to pay the balloon. You offer to extend the payment if the payer will agree to boost the interest rate to say 15%. If they payer agrees, you have solved one problem and yet created another. You originally made 15% by the combination of the discount paid by the seller and a stated interest rate paid by the payer. Now the payer is paying the entire 15%, which may be over the legal limit.

Usury Problems With the Seller

There are two problem areas with usury that involve the seller. The first problem arises when the seller guarantees the payments on the note. This happens automatically unless the seller endorsed the note "without recourse." If the payer fails to make the payments, the seller becomes responsible and you seek payment from the seller. However, this may backfire because of a usury problem. You then are demanding that the seller pay you both the discount and the stated rate of interest on the note, which may exceed the usury statutes. If considered usurious under state law, the seller could sue you for usury and prevail in a legal action. The solution is to only buy notes endorsed "without recourse" which does not obligate the seller to guarantee the note.

Partial Purchases

The second problem with the seller arises when you do not buy all of the note. This is sometimes called a "partial purchase." For example, the note may take 120 months to pay off. You purchase the next 60 payments and make an agreement to return the note to the seller after you have received your 60 payments. Many sellers think that they are borrowing money from you; despite the fact your agreement may clearly state that this is a sale. There is a serious question as to whether this is a sale or a loan. The judicial decisions are not final in this area.

To avoid legal problems, please be sure to retain legal counsel concerning usury laws.

Checking Out The Down Payment

In a typical seller financed note transaction, the amount of the down payment has a direct effect on the security for the note. The greater the down payment, the less the risk you have that the payer will fail to make his payment and leave you with a delinquent note.

An important concept defined by lenders is the "loan to value ratio" (LTV). The lower the LTV, the greater the chances of receiving timely payments. How do you calculate the LTV? For example, if a seller sold a house for $100,000, with a $60,000 down payment and carried a note back for the $40,000 balance, the LTV would be 40%. This relatively large down payment would be comfortable for you as a note holder. If the payer defaults, there would be a 60% equity cushion for recovery of your money.

On the other hand, if a seller sold a house for $100,000 with a $5,000 down payment, the resulting 95% LTV would not give you a sufficient margin for recovery in the event of a default. After paying attorney's fees, fix up costs, marketing expenses, and commissions, there would be insufficient funds to you to recover your investment.

Investment to Value Ratio

The most important concept relative to the evaluation of down payments is referred to as the "investment to value ratio" (ITV). ITV is the amount you pay for a note as a percentage of the total value of the property. For example, if the property sold for $100,000 with a $10,000 down payment and a $90,000 note, the LTV is 90%. If you purchased the note, however, at a discount for $60,000, your ITV is only 60% giving you a significant cushion over the LTV.

Even if you're able to purchase the note at a discount resulting in a favorable ITV, the high LTV may still be a significant risk for you simply because the payer has little at stake and may default on the note.

If there is a down payment of less that 20% of the purchase price, it should behoove you to ask questions and to seek further verification of the transaction details. You might consider whether the payer is financially strong enough to make a larger down payment or whether the payer doesn't have a big financial stake in the transaction, or whether the property may have been overpriced at the time of the sale.

Larger Than Normal Down Payment

A larger than normal down payment should also trigger some serious and probing questions. If the down payment is larger than 30%-35%, you might consider some of the following questions for further inquiry:

(1)   Why wasn't a traditional lender used for the balance of the purchase price if such a large down payment were made?

(2)   Was the down payment borrowed so that the payer now has two loans to pay off.

(3)   Was the down payment actually made at all?

Verifying The Down Payment

Unfortunately, in most cases, the seller does not verify the source of the down payment prior to selling the property. It is often times difficult to verify that source.

There are several sources available to determine whether the payer actually made the down payment and whether the down payment was in cash or in some other form.

One of the most significant items used to verify the down payment is the purchaser's closing statement. This statement indicates that a down payment was made and the other expenses and charges relating to the purchase of the property. Sometimes these closing statements are difficult to obtain, since the payer doesn't benefit financially from your purchase of the note. Insist upon obtaining a copy of the closing statement from the seller of the note or in many instances, copies can be obtained with no difficulty from the closing attorney.

Be wary of the extra cooperative payer or a closing statement which indicated that down payments were made outside of closing. You will typically see this on a closing statement as "POC" which means paid outside of closing.

Canceled checks are the best proof that a cash down payment was actually made. The payer is most likely to have copies of the canceled checks. However, the payer must cooperate with you in providing the copies of the checks.

One of the best sources to obtain verification is from the closing agent or the attorney who distributed money at the time the property was sold. The real estate agent who received the earnest money is also a likely source. Closing agents, attorneys, and real estate brokers often make copies of funds prior to depositing them into their trust accounts. These professionals can also order copies of the canceled checks from the bank. Although this may be a time consuming and expensive proposition, it is well worth the effort for you.

There are several indirect sources from which you can derive further information.

For example, a credit report from a payer can assist you in verifying the credibility of the transaction. You need to check so see if the payer's credit history is consistent with the amount of the purported down payment. If it is not, you need to question where the down payment really did come from. Also, verify the prior addresses of the payer, which show a relationship with the seller, which may raise the possibility of fraud or collusion.

Also verify the written appraisal of the property. If the appraised value of the property is not in line with the purchase price, the down payment may be overstated or manufactured. Public records can sometimes give you a clue as to the actual value or sales price of the property. An easy way to determine what the actual sales price was is to examine the transfer tax stamp attached to the recorded deed of transfer. In the state of Georgia the state transfer tax is currently $1 per $1,000 of the purchase price. Therefore, if you saw a $100 tax stamp on the warranty deed, it would indicate that the purchase price would be $100,000.

Proof of Payments

Payments on seller financed notes are normally collected either by an agent or directly by the seller. Example: an escrow company, title insurance company, contract collection agency, accountant, lawyer, real estate company, or bank; there is usually no problem about reliable payment history. These companies and individuals have specialized equipment and professional standards that prevent exaggeration or alteration of information about payments.

However, when the seller is self-collecting the payments directly from the payer, difficulty arises. The seller may keep the payment records that range all the way from solid proof of payment to no proof at all. The best possible payment record would be a complete set of the payer's canceled checks. However, it is unlikely that the seller would have the payer's canceled checks because they belong to the payer. You may ask the payer for them, but don't expect to obtain them because the payer might not have kept canceled checks or may not wish to cooperate with the seller. Also, this would alert the payer that a sale of the note was about to take place and you might find yourself in a position where the payer will commence negotiation with the note holder to buy the note at a discount.

There is one possible way to obtain the payer's cancelled checks even if he refuses to supply copies. If the seller deposited the payer's checks into the seller's bank account, copies of the canceled checks would be available at a fee from the seller's bank. However, this normally takes a great deal of time and can be quite expensive.

A seller can sometimes provide you with copies of their bank statements, which show deposits of the payer's payments. The seller may not want you to review bank statements for reasons of privacy.

Many self-collecting sellers will present a sheet of paper recording dates and amounts and principal and interest breakdown, or a book with the same information. Likewise, many sellers will provide a copy of an amortization schedule at the time the property was obtained by the payer and on which check marks, initials, and dates have been entered as the payments were made.

Many sellers think that providing a notarized affidavit, affirming that they have received all payments, constitutes proof of payment. This is simply not the case. A notary does not check the truth of what the seller says but only establishes the seller's identity correctly.

When the note goes into default or
(when the note goes to hell in a hand basket)

When the note goes into default, it is important that you be aware of not only the legal choices you have but also the practical choices that you may want to pursue.

It is always best to work out some amicable solution with the payer who is facing default. There may be many cases in which the payer has encountered some temporary problem or condition, which may resolve itself. For example, if the payer has temporarily lost a job, been involved in an accident, or something that may remedy itself it the future, then it is best to work with the payer if possible.

This could take the form of doing nothing. Adding the past due payments at the end of the note as principal, or restructuring the note by utilizing one of the methods that we have previously discussed.

If you do amend the note, it is critical that you have a competent attorney to document the changes. If you are a senior lien holder, it is prudent to get the junior lien holder's permission for these changes to protect your lien's seniority.

There are various legal remedies available as final options towards enforcing your rights. When there is a default and no amiable solution can be reached, your choices in dealing with the default are: 1) sue on the note, 2) foreclose on the property, 3) take a deed to the property in lieu of foreclosure.

If you choose to sue only on the note, there are several alternatives. The payer may have other assets that could be attached to pay the debt, in addition to the property. You may not want the property, which secures the note. If you have a valid promissory note, it should be quite easy, in most instances, to obtain a judgment against the payer. In that regard, if a judgment is obtained, then it becomes a general lien against all of the payer's property and assets.

In the State of Georgia, property is foreclosed upon by the method known as non-judicial foreclosure. This means that the property is advertised for sale once a week for four weeks prior to the judicial sale, which takes place on the first Tuesday of each month. In non-judicial foreclosure states such as Georgia, it is not necessary to go to court, file a lawsuit, and obtain a judgment against the payer prior to foreclosing on the property.

In those states such as Florida which have a judicial foreclosure preceding, it is incumbent upon you as a note holder to obtain competent legal counsel to file the appropriate proceedings and advise you accordingly. This is a legal proceeding and you should not undertake to do this on your own. There is an old saying that a man who represents himself in his own legal proceeding, has a fool for a lawyer and an idiot for a client.

What should you do in the event that the property, which has been foreclosed upon, does not bring the full value of the note and costs associated with the foreclosure? In the State of Georgia, we have what is known as a confirmation proceeding. This means that the foreclosing party would have to bring a legal proceeding in the Superior Court to obtain a deficiency judgment against the payer if the property did not bring its full value. These proceedings have very strict legal requirements, and require the assistance of competent legal counsel.

Another method of dealing with defaults is to take a deed in lieu of foreclosure. This method is the fastest and least expensive.

By utilizing this procedure, the note holder takes immediate control over the property and the cost of foreclosure can be avoided. However, one should be very careful to conduct a title search scrutinizing all the liens against the property prior to taking a deed in lieu of foreclosure. If there are additional liens, or federal or state tax liens, or property tax liens, then you might be taking the property subject to these liens.

There is also the possibility that the payer might declare bankruptcy, either Chapter 7 or Chapter 13. The bankruptcy proceedings create many delays and costly legal entanglements that you want to avoid if possible. You must be warned that if you accept a deed in lieu of foreclosure, the bankruptcy court may reverse it, citing preferential treatment and setting aside the conveyance.

You must always be aware of the fact that once an individual files bankruptcy, you should avoid any contact with the individual until further notice of the court. Always deal with the bankrupt parties' attorney or through the court's trustee. Otherwise, you might find yourself in contempt proceedings in the federal bankruptcy court. Again, it is advisable that you seek competent legal counsel if this event occurs.

Notes:

The Foreclosure Process

In a judicial foreclosure, the mortgagee files a lawsuit against the mortgagor in the proper court to foreclose on the property. The case is then set for trial. If the court rules in favor of the mortgagee, the property will be ordered sold at a public sale. In most instances, however, there is a non-judicial foreclosure. In a non-judicial foreclosure, the court system is not involved. To foreclose non-judicially, the mortgage must contain a power of sale clause. The power of sale clause gives the mortgagee the right to begin foreclosure without going to court. To include a power of sale clause does not require a specific form or language.

If, on the other hand, the security instrument does not contain a power of sale provision, judicial foreclosure is the mortgagee's only way to obtain the property. Most conventional mortgages say "with the power of sale".

Judicial and non-judicial foreclosures differ in many ways. The foreclosure method selected by the mortgagee has significant consequences .

Non judicial foreclosure is relatively fast, as this method does not involve the court system. In most instances, non-judicial foreclosure takes, at minimum, about four months after the mortgagor has failed to meet the obligation or defaulted on the loan. Judicial foreclosure, on the other hand, may take up to several years.

Non judicial foreclosure is generally less costly than judicial foreclosure. In a non-judicial foreclosure, the mortgagee's and attorney's fees are largely specified by law. In a judicial foreclosure, however, there are generally no legal limits for attorney's fees. As a result, the mortgagor may be liable for significant legal expenses.

Another major difference between the two foreclosure methods is the mortgagee's right to a deficiency judgment. A deficiency judgment is a court order stating that the mortgagor still owes money to the beneficiary if the proceeds from the foreclosure sale are not sufficient to pay the balance of the debt.

State laws also differ with regard to the mortgagor's right of redemption after the foreclosure sale. This is the mortgagor's right to reclaim the foreclosure property. In some states such as Georgia, the sale of the property at the foreclosure sale is an irrevocable final sale, and the mortgagor does not have the right to redeem or reclaim the property after the sale.

This summary of the major differences between non-judicial and judicial foreclosure shows the advantages of non-judicial foreclosure for the mortgagee. The non-judicial foreclosure is timely, economical, not subject to redemption, and may command a higher sales price. In addition, it is unlikely that the mortgagee would recover any losses through a deficiency judgment, as the mortgagor could not make the loan payments in the first place.

Notes:

_____

_____

_____

_____

_____

_____

_____

_____

_____

_____

Glossary of Real Estate Financial Terms

Abstract of Title - A summary of all the recorded instruments and proceedings that affect the title to property, arranged in the order in which they were recorded.

Accelerate - To make a debt due and payable at once.

Acceleration Clause - A provision in a note, mortgage or trust deed that permits the holder to declare the entire unpaid balance due and payable at once upon the happening of some particular event, such as failure to pay an installment on time or sale of the property used as security.

Accrued interest - Interest that has been earned but is not due and payable.

Acknowledgment - A formal declaration before an authorized official (usually a notary public) by the person who executed a document stating that he did in fact execute it. The notary public signs and puts his seal on a written statement describing the declaration. This written statement, or acknowledgment, is required on most instruments before they may be recorded.

All-Inclusive Contract of Sale, Mortgage or Trust Deed - See Wrap-Around Contract of Sale, Mortgage or Trust Deed.

ALTA Title Insurance Policy - A type of title insurance issued to lenders that gives greater coverage than a standard policy by insuring against additional items, such as unrecorded physical easements, unrecorded mechanic's liens, water and mineral rights, facts a physical survey would not show, and rights of persons in possession. Formerly called ATA title insurance policy. ALTA is an abbreviation for American Land Title Association, a trade association of title insurance companies.

Amortization - The repayment of a debt in installments.

Amortized Loan - A loan that is completely paid off in installments.

Amortized Note - A promissory note that is completely paid off in installments.

Annual Statement - A statement required by some state statues to be given by a note holder to the payer within 60 days after the end of each year itemizing and accounting for the money received during the year just ended.

Appraisal Report - The report, written by a real estate appraiser, stating the appraiser's opinion of the value of real property.

Appraised Value - An estimate or opinion of value at a stated time. The opinion of value expressed by a real estate professional known as a real estate appraiser.

Assessed Value -The value placed on property for taxation purposes.

Assessor - An official who has the responsibility of determining assessed value.

Assign - To transfer title to personal property or a right or claim to another person.

Assignee - A person to whom title to personal property or a right or claim is transferred.

Assignment - A transfer by one person (the assignor) to another (the assignee) of title to personal property.

Assignor - A person who transfers title to personal property or a right or claim to another person.

Assume - To take over the obligation of another, for example, to assume a note and deed of trust.

Assumption Agreement - An agreement under which a person (usually a buyer) "assumes" (that is, agrees to pay) a note and mortgage or deed of trust on a property.

Balloon Payment - A final installment payment, larger than previous installments, that pays off a debt.

Bene Statement - See Beneficiary Statement.

Beneficiary - The person entitled to the benefit of a trust. In a trust deed the beneficiary is the creditor who is secured and for whose benefit the trustee holds legal title.

Beneficiary Statement - A statement by the holder of a deed of trust stating the amount of the unpaid principal on the note and other information about the debt. The holder is required to give this statement upon payment of a small fee. Also called an offset statement or a bene statement.

Blanket Mortgage or Blanket Trust Deed - A mortgage or deed of trust covering more than one piece of property. For example, it may cover an entire subdivision and provide for a partial reconveyance of individual lots as they are sold.

Call - to declare the entire debt due at once.

Certificate of Discharge - A written instrument executed by the mortgagee and given to the mortgagor when the debt secured by a mortgage is satisfied to show that the mortgage is released. Sometimes called a release of mortgage.

Certificate of Sale - A certificate issued to the buyer at an execution sale or judicial foreclosure sale. The holder of the certificate is entitled to a deed if the owner of the property does not redeem it within 1 year in some states.

Closing Statement - A statement from an escrow agent given to the parties at closing when it is closed, accounting for all funds received into and paid out of escrow.

Collateral - Property used as security for a debt.

Collateral Assignment - An assignment of property for security purposes rather than absolute assignment.

Community Property - Property acquired by a husband and wife while married and not separated, except property acquired by gift, will, or inheritance and certain other items specified by statute. Any other property owned by a husband or wife is separate property.

Comparison Approach - See Market Data Approach.

Compound Interest - Interest computed not only on the principal but also on previously accumulated interest.

Conditional Sale - A contract for the sale of property stating that although delivery is to be made to the buyer, the title is to remain vested in the seller until the conditions of the contract have been fulfilled.

Conditional Sales Contract - See Land Contract.

Consideration - Anything of value given to induce another party to enter into a contract.

Contract - An agreement between two or more parties to do or not to do certain things for the breach of which the law will give a remedy.

Contract for Deed - See Land Contract.

Contract of Sale - See Land Contract.

Conventional Loan - A loan made without government guarantee.

Conveyance - A written instrument that transfers title to or an interest in real property.

Corporation - An artificial person, created by law that has certain powers and duties of a natural person.

Cosigner - A person who signs a note as an additional maker to help another maker secure a loan.

Cost Basis - The aggregate amount an owner pays to acquire an asset plus all capital improvements, if any, less capital losses and depreciation taken.

Credit Report - A report on a credit applicant from a credit reporting service stating creditors' experience with the applicant and frequently containing information or estimates about the applicant's assets, liabilities and character.

Creditor - A person to whom a debt is owed.

Current Value - The value at the time of appraisal.

Debt Financing - The use of borrowed capital to finance the purchase of property.

Debt Service - The sum of money needed each month or year to amortize a loan.

Debtor - A person who owes a debt.

Declining Principal Loan - A loan for which interest is calculated each month, quarter, etc., on the remaining balance of the loan.

Deed - A written instrument transferring title to real property from one person to another.

Deed of Reconveyance - See Reconveyance Deed.

Deed Of Trust - A written instrument transferring bare legal title to real property to a trustee to be held as security for an obligation. Also called a trust deed. The accepted form is presented to the trustee for approval before the execution thereof by the trustor and beneficiary and before recordation. The trustee is therefore duty-bound to perform if he accepts. The automatic form is the most widely used form. It contains a provision whereby the trustee named will accept his duties when the trust deed is properly executed, acknowledged, and recorded and provided he has approved the promissory note and deed of trust. The trustee is not usually aware of the appointment until called on to act in case of default by the trustor.

Default - Failure to fulfill a duty or promise, or to discharge an obligation; omission, or failure to perform an act. In property foreclosure, usually the failure to pay loan installment payments when they become due.

Defeasance Clause - A provision in a mortgage that allows the mortgagor to have his property released from the mortgage when the secured debt is paid.

Deficiency Judgment - A judgment for the amount left unpaid after a property has been sold at a foreclosure sale when the net proceeds are not sufficient to pay off the loan.

Demand Note - A note that is payable on demand of the holder.

Discount - (1) To sell a note for less than the unpaid balance due on it. (2) The dollar difference between the unpaid balance of a note and the price for which a note holder sells the note.

Discount Interest - Interest that is deducted from the principal amount of the loan in advance by the lender on the first day of the loan, hence increasing the lender's yield.

Discount Points - A fee, expressed as a percentage of the loan amount, when making a loan. Points increase the yield.

Dragnet Clause - A clause in a deed of trust that makes it security not only for the present loan but also for any other past or future debts to the beneficiary.

Due-On-Sale Clause - A clause in a note or deed of trust giving the holder the right to declare the entire debt due and payable if the owner sells or contracts to sell the property. Also called a due-on-alienation clause.

Effective Interest Rate - The actual rate of interest the borrower pays in interest for his loan. Also called true interest rate.

Encumbrance - In a legal or technical sense, anything that limits or affects the ownership of property, such as a lien, mortgage, easement or restriction. In the daily language of real estate people, the term usually means a lien.

Endorsement - A signature placed on the back of a note or check to transfer ownership. An endorsement in blank guarantees payment to later holders. An endorsement without recourse, or qualified endorsement, does not guarantee payment to later holders.

Entity - A form of business organization.

Equitable Title - The ownership held by a buyer after he has contracted to buy property but before legal title has been conveyed to him.

Equity in Property - The current market value of a property less the amount of all liens and charges against it.

Equity Loan - Junior (subordinate) loan based on a percentage of the equity.

Equity of Redemption - (1) The right of an owner to redeem his property after he has defaulted on a mortgage. (2) In some states the term is usually applied to the right of an owner to redeem his property for 1 year after judicial foreclosure sale. Also called right of redemption.

Equity Return or Buildup - Dollars paid towards the principal on a loan that reduces the outstanding balance.

Escalation - The raising of some item, such as the interest rate or size of installment payments. The right to escalate the interest rate or size of payment may be given by contract to the lender under specified conditions.

Escalator Clause - A clause providing that an item will be adjusted upward or downward under certain conditions. For example, a note may provide that the interest rate goes up or down as the cost of living index rises or falls.

Escrow: - The deposit of items such as money, deeds, and other instruments by contracting parties with a neutral party, called an escrow holder or escrow agent, to be held until all the terms and conditions of the escrow agreement are fulfilled. Then there is a close of escrow, and the items are delivered to the respective parties entitled to them.

Escrow Officer - An employee of an escrow agent who has the responsibility of handling and closing escrows.

Estoppel Certificate - An instrument executed by a note payer setting forth the status of and the balance due on the promissory note as of the date of the execution of the certificate.

Extension Agreement - An agreement giving additional time in which to pay money or perform some other obligation.

Fee- The fullest estate a person may own in real property. It is the estate almost all owners hold. Also called fee simple.

Fictitious Deed of Trust - A trust deed recorded by a trustee that does not cover an actual transaction. The trustee may then in later deeds of trust refer to the fictitious trust deed and incorporate its terms without repeating them in the part of the trust deed being recorded. This saves recording fees.

Finance Change - The total dollar amount of all charges and interest the lender will make to the borrower over the life of the loan. Includes everything except principal.

Finder's Fee - A fee agreed to be paid to one person, called a finder, who locates another person, such as a buyer or lender, desired by the party promising to pay the fee. The fee is payable when the deal is consummated. In real estate transactions the finder may introduce the parties, but in some states he may not engage in negotiations unless he holds a real estate broker's, mortgage brokers, or a real estate salesman's license.

First Lien - The debt instrument recorded first (earliest in time) such as a first mortgage or first deed of trust. This debt has priority as a lien over all other debts. In cases of foreclosure, the first lien will be satisfied before other liens are paid off.

Foreclosure - The procedure of enforcing a lien by the sale of the property covered by the lien.

Foreclosure Sale - The sale of property in a foreclosure. Most often, it is the sale of the property securing a debt after default in payment.

Free and Clear - Free means a freehold estate, and in this expression it means a fee title. Clear means there are no money encumbrances against the property. Generally used to refer to a property free of mortgage debt.

Future Advance - Money loaned to a borrower after the execution of a trust deed under a clause making the trust deed security for such later advances. Obligatory future advances are those the lender is required to make under his contract with the borrower. Non obligatory future advances are those the lender is not required to make.

Grace Period - Additional time allowed to perform an act or make a payment before default occurs.

Grant - A term used in deeds of conveyance to indicate a transfer of real property.

Grantee - The party to whom the title to real property is conveyed by deed; the buyer.

Grantor - The party who conveys real property by deed; the seller.

Gross Profit Percentage - Realized gain on the sale or exchange of real property divided by the net sales price of the property. Used to multiply by each year's principal received on a purchase money note to calculate the recognized gain for the year for tax reporting.

Hard Money - (I) Cash loaned: contrasted with soft money, which means credit extended rather than cash. These expressions are often encountered in such a term as hard-money trust deed. (2) Some people use this term to mean a high-interest loan.

Hazard Insurance - Insurance against damage to property from physical hazard, such as fire and windstorm.

Holder in Due Course- A person who takes a negotiable instrument, such as a note or check in good faith for value before it is past due and without notice of any defects when it was negotiated to him. Certain defenses that the maker could have claimed against the original payee, such as payment in full or in part, or certain types of fraud cannot be claimed against a holder in due course.

Hypothecation - Giving real or personal property as security without parting with possession.

Installment Contract - See Land Contract.

Installment Note - A promissory note calling for periodic payments.

Installments - Parts of the same debt, payable at successive periods as agreed.

Institutional lender - An institution that makes substantial numbers of real estate loans such as a bank, a savings and loan association or an insurance company.

Instrument - A writing executed as the expression of some contract, act or proceeding; for example, a deed.

Insurable Interest - An interest in property such that damage to the property would cause the owner of the interest a financial loss; for example, the interest of a tenant or the holder of a trust deed.

Interest - (1) Legally, any charge a lender or creditor makes for the use, forbearance or detention of money, no matter how the charge is labeled by the parties. (2) In daily usage, the percentage charged by the lender.

Interest-Only Loan or Note - A loan or note for which the installment payments are 100% interest; thus the payments do not reduce the principal balance of the loan or note.

Interest Rate - The charge made for a loan of money or use of credit, expressed as a percentage of the principal.

Investment-to-value Ratio - When purchasing a note and deed of trust, the amount invested in the note plus the current unpaid balances of all senior loans divided by the current market value or appraised value of the property securing the loans. Investment-to-value ratio is usually expressed as a percentage.

Involuntary Lien - A lien imposed on property without the consent of the owner; for example, real property taxes and judgment liens.

Joint Note - A note in which there are two or more makers who share equal liability on it.

Joint Tenancy - Ownership of property by two or more persons, each of whom has an undivided interest with the right of survivorship.

Joint Venture - A business entity composed of two or more people joined together to conduct a single enterprise for profit. It is treated legally almost like a partnership, but differs from a partnership by having as its objects a single venture instead of a continuing business.

Judgment - A final determination by a court of law. Most often, a judgment is for a sum of money.

Judicial Foreclosure - Foreclosure through court.

Junior Lien - An inferior or subordinate lien. For example, a second deed of trust is a junior to a first trust deed.

Land Contract - A security device used in the sale of real property. The buyer contracts to pay the purchase price in installments. The seller contracts that when the purchase price is paid in full, he will deed the property to the buyer. Until the purchase price is paid in full, the seller keeps legal title. Also called conditional sales contract, contract for deed, contract of sale.

Late Charge - A specified charge added by a creditor under his note or contract when the debtor makes his payment late or after a certain date.

Legal Description - A description of real estate sufficient to allow a competent surveyor to locate the property on the ground.

Level Payments - Payments of equal size.

Lien - A legal right or claim upon a specific property that attaches to the property until the debt is satisfied.

Lien Release - A written agreement by a lien holder releasing the debtor from further obligation.

Limited Partnership - A special type of partnership with one or more general partners who manage the business and are responsible for its debts, and one or more limited partners who take no part in its management and are not responsible for its debts.

Loan-to-Value Ratio - The sum of current unpaid loan balances for all loans against a property divided by the current market value or appraised value of the property securing the loans. Loan -to-value ratio is usually expressed as a percentage.

Lock-in-Clause - A clause in a note, mortgage or trust deed setting a period during which no prepayment is allowed on the loan.

MAI - A designation for a member of the American Institute of appraisers, a part of the National Association of Realtors. The initials stand for Member of American Institute.

Maker - The person who signs a note agreeing to pay it. Also called the payer.

Market Data Approach - An appraisal technique based on sales of comparable properties. Also called comparison approach.

Market Price - The price paid regardless of motives, pressures or intelligence.

Market Value - The highest price, estimated in terms of money, that property would bring if exposed for sale in the open market, allowing a reasonable time to find a buyer who buys with full knowledge of all the uses to which the property is adapted and all the uses for which it is capable of being used.

Mechanic's Lien - A lien given by statute to persons supplying labor, materials or services to improve real property. To perfect the lien, certain notices and recordings are required.

Mortgage - An instrument in writing, duly executed and delivered, that creates a lien upon real estate as security for the payment of a specified debt.

Mortgage Money Market - The source of financing for real estate. It is divided into two parts: The primary mortgage money market consists of all the sources of loans made directly by lenders; the secondary mortgage money market consists of all buyers of existing real estate loans as collateral.

Mortgage Reduction Certificate - An instrument executed by the mortgagee, setting forth the status of and the balance due on the mortgage as of the date of the execution of the instrument.

Mortgagee - The party who lends money and takes a mortgage to secure payment.

Mortgagor - A person who borrows money and gives a mortgage on his or her property as security for the payment of the debt.

Negotiable Instrument - An instrument, such as a check or note, that meets certain legal requirements that allow it to be transferred free of most claims the maker had against previous holders.

Nominal Interest Rate - The rate of interest stated in a note or contract. This may not be the true or effective rate (actual cost) to the borrower.

Non institutional Lender - A lender that is not an institution, such as retirement funds, endowed universities, and private individuals.

Non-judicial Foreclosure - A foreclosure by having property sold to satisfy the debt without going through court.

Notary Public - A person empowered to administer oaths and to attest or certify documents to assure their authenticity.

Note - An instrument in which one party, the maker or payer, promises to pay a definite sum of money to another, the payee, at a fixed or determinable future time or on demand.

Notice of Default - A notice that is recorded and is given to certain people entitled to it stating that a trust deed is in default and that the trust deed holder has chosen to have the property sold. This notice starts the running of a grace period during which the property owner can cure the default by paying up the debt that is past due.

Notice of Trustee's Sale - A notice provided by law requiring the trustee to advertise the property in default in a newspaper of general circulation.

Obligee - A person to whom a legal obligation or duty is owed; for example, the payee of a note.

Obligor- A person who has placed himself under a legal obligation; for example, the maker of a note.

Offset Statement - See Beneficiary Statement.

Open-End Clause - A clause that permits the outstanding balance of the loan to be increased by the borrower under the provisions outlined in the agreement.

Open End Deed of Trust or Mortgage - A trust deed or mortgage that secures not only that original debt but also future advances made after the date of the trust deed or mortgage.

Option - A Contract that gives one party (the optionee) the right to enter into some type of contract upon specified terms with another party (the optionor). Usually, the right to buy the optionor's property or note for a particular price.

Package Deed of Trust or Mortgage - A trust deed or mortgage secured by both real property and personal property.

Partial Reconveyance - A reconveyance that releases a part but not all of a tract from the lien of a trust deed or mortgage.

Partial Release Clause - A provision in a trust deed, mortgage or land contract that permits the borrower or buyer to secure the release of part of the property by complying with certain terms, such as the payment of a certain sum of money.

Partnership - A voluntary association of two or more persons to carry on business for profit.

Payee - A person to whom a note states it is payable.

Payer - A person who signs a note agreeing to pay it. Also called a maker.

Point -1 % of the principal amount of a loan. A lender often charges points when a loan is made, renewed or assumed, to raise the yield on the loan.

Power -of-Sale Clause - A clause in trust deeds and in some mortgages giving the trustee or mortgagee the right to sell the property that is security for the loan at public sale, without court procedure, if the debtor defaults.

Preliminary Title Insurance Report - A report by a title insurance company showing the condition of title to a property including liens, restrictions, etc.

Prepayment - To pay off all or part of a debt before it is due.

Prepayment Clause - A provision in a note or deed of trust allowing the borrower to pay off all or part of the principal before it is due, with or without a prepayment penalty.

Prepayment Penalty - A charge provided in a note or deed of trust for the privilege of paying all or part of the debt before it is due.

Primary Financing - The loan which has first priority; the loan which has its security instrument recorded first.

Primary Mortgage Money Market - See Mortgage Money Market.

Principal - The capital amount of a loan, not including interest. The principal portion of an installment payment on a loan reduces the outstanding balance of the loan by the amount of the principal payment.

Principal Plus Interest Loan - A loan for which the borrower makes a fixed principal payment each period and pays, in addition, interest on the unpaid principal amount of the loan.

Promissory Note - See Note.

Purchase Money Deed of Trust or Mortgage - A trust deed or mortgage given to secure all or part of the purchase price of real estate.

Quitclaim Deed - A deed that conveys simply the grantor's rights or interest in real estate; generally considered inadequate except when interests are being passed from one spouse to the other.

Rate of Return - See Yield Rate.

Realized Gain - Total profit on the sale or exchange of real property. Computed as net sales price less cost basis.

Real Property - Land and things attached to the land, such as buildings and other appurtenances.

Recognized Gain - The amount of the realized gain on the sale or exchange of real property reportable in a given year on tax returns.

Reconveyance Deed - A deed from a trustee under a trust deed conveying legal title back to the property owner to release the lien of the trust deed. Also called a deed of reconveyance.

Recordation - The recording of an instrument in the county recorder's office to give constructive notice of it.

Recourse - The right to claim against a prior owner of a property or note.

Redemption - (1) The correcting of a default under a trust deed or mortgage by paying the entire indebtedness plus foreclosure costs. (2) The reacquiring (buying back) of property sold at a judicial foreclosure sale by paying the amount for which it was sold plus certain other items specified by statute. See also Equity of Redemption.

Refinance - To obtain new financing to pay off an existing loan.

Reinstatement - The curing of a default under a trust deed or mortgage by paying up the amount past due. Reinstatement restores the loan to the status it had before the default.

Release Clause - A provision in a blanket mortgage or trust deed allowing the owner of the properties to secure the release of properties upon certain terms, usually the payment of a certain sum of money.

Release of Liability - A letter or other form of release that relieves a debtor of any further responsibility on his debt or other obligation.

Release of Mortgage - A written instrument releasing the lien of a mortgage on real property. See also Certificate of Discharge.

Request for Reconveyance - An instrument executed by a trust deed holder directing the trustee to convey legal title to the property involved back to the owner. Most often, a form for this request is printed on the back of the trust deed so that the creditor may execute it when the debt is satisfied. Nevertheless, it may also be a separate instrument.

Rescind - To cancel a contract or other transaction and restore to each what he had given under it.

Rescission - (I) The act of rescinding. (2) A legal action to rescind a contract or other transaction.

Restriction - A limitation upon the use of property that is specified in the title deed.

Return - See Yield.

Right of Redemption - See Equity of Redemption.

Right of Survivorship - Right of the surviving joint owner to succeed to the interest of the deceased joint owner.

Satisfaction - Performance of the terms of a contract, usually by payment in full of an obligation.

Satisfied - Paid or performed in full.

Second Loan - A loan secured by a second deed of trust or mortgage.

Secondary Mortgage Money Market - See Mortgage Money Market.

Secured Party - The person for whose benefit security is given.

Set-Off - A claim a debtor is entitled to make against a creditor that reduces or eliminates the amount the debtor owed the creditor.

Simple Interest - Interest computed on the unpaid principal amount of the loan without provisions for additional interest to be paid on interest.

Soft Money - Credit extended as opposed to cash (hard money). Also, see Purchase Money Deed of Trust or Mortgage.

Straight Note - A promissory note with the principal payable in one lump sum instead of in installments.

Stipulations - The terms within a written contract.

Subordination - The act of making an existing loan secondary or junior to another lien or loan.

Subordination Agreement - A contract by which the holder of a prior lien makes it junior or inferior to another lien.

Substitution of Mortgagor - An agreement in which the lender on a loan being assumed by buyer agrees to relieve the original borrower of liability.

Substitution of Trustee -An instrument that the beneficiary under a trust deed executes and records to substitute a new trustee for an earlier one.

Tenancy in Common - An ownership of real property by two or more persons, each of whom has an undivided interest, without right of survivorship.

Term - A provision of a loan or contract that specifies the length of time the contract is to run.

Title - Evidence of the ownership of real property.

Title Company - Firm examining title to real property and/or issuing title insurance.

Title Defect - Unresolved claim against the ownership of property that prevents presentation of a marketable title. Such claims may arise from failure of the owner's spouse, or former part owner, to sign a deed, current liens against the property, or an interruption in the title records of a property.

Title Insurance - Insurance that protects against loss because of faulty title.

Title Report - Document indicating the current state of the title, such as easements, covenants, liens and any other defects. The title report does not describe the chain of title. See also Abstract of Title.

Title Search - An examination of the public records to determine ownership and encumbrances affecting real property.

Trust Deed - See Deed of Trust.

Trustee - A person who holds bare legal title to real or personal property for the benefit of another person. A trustee is one of the parties in a trust deed.

Trustee's Deed - A deed issued to the successful bidder at a trustee's sale. A trustee's deed conveys title to the purchaser free and clear, but subject to all senior liens.

Trustor – A person who conveys property to a trustee. In a trust deed the trustor is the borrower or debtor.

Undivided Interest – Ownership of real estate by joint tenants or tenants in common under the same title.

Unsecured – Without security.

Usury - The charging of more interest than is allowed by law.

Valid - Having force, or binding force; legally sufficient and authorized by law.

Valuation - Estimated worth or price. The act of valuing by appraisal.

Vendee - A buyer.

Vendee's Lien - A lien against real property under a land contract to secure a deposit paid by a purchaser

Vendor - A seller.

Void - (1) Having no legal effect; null. (2) To have an instrument transaction declared void.

Voidable - That which is capable of being adjudged void, but is not void unless action is taken to make it so.

Voluntary Lien – A lien intentionally put on real property by the owner.

Waiver - The renunciation, abandonment or surrender of some claim, right or privilege.

Warranty Deed - A conveyance of real property in which the grantor guarantees the title to the grantee.

Without Recourse - Words used endorsing a note to denote that the future holder is not to look to the endorser in case of non-payment.

Wrap-Around Contract of Sale, Mortgage or Trust Deed - A land contract, mortgage, or trust deed that works like this: The debtor owns or buys property with a first deed of trust seller on it. A seller or second lender takes a second deed of trust or second mortgage or a land contract for an amount that includes not only the amount owed to this second party but also the amount of the first trust deed. The owner makes one monthly payment to this second party. Out of it the second party makes the payment on the first trust deed and keeps the rest as his payment. Also called all- inclusive contract of sale, mortgage or trust deed.

Yield - Interest earned by the lender on the money loaned. Also called return.

Yield Rate - Yield expressed as a percentage of the total investment. Also called rate of return.

Illustrations

Free Purchase Quotation For Note Holders

If you are interested in the possibility of selling all or part of your note for cash, and would like to know how much your note is worth, please fill out the following information and send this form or a photo copy to:

E. Wright Davis
339 Brookside Court
Palm Harbor, Florida 34683
E-Mail: ewrightdavis@verizon.net

Original face amount of note: _____

Annual interest rate: _____ Original number of payments due: _____

Frequency of payments (monthly, quarterly, etc.): _____

Payment amount: _____ Date of first payment: _____

Number of remaining payments: _____ Are payments current?: _____

Amount and date of balloon payment, if any: _____

Current balance, if known: _____

Balance(s) of underlying loans, if any: _____

Priority of your note (1st, 2", etc.): _____

Type of property securing note: _____

Street Address of property: _____

City:_____ State: _____ Zip: _____

Date of sale of property: _____ Sale price of property: _____

Cash down payment you received: _____

Your estimate of the market value of the property: _____

Instead of filling out the above information you can send us copies of the note, deed of trust and closing statement you received when you sold your property and we will gather the needed information. *Please rush me a quotation on the purchase of my note. Include several full and partial purchase options.*

Name: _____

Street Address: _____

City:_____ State: _____ Zip: _____

Phone: _____(In case we have questions)

Cash Flows You Might Not Know About

Here are cash flows to buy and broker that most people have never thought of. Specializing in an area that few if any are working can be very profitable indeed:

Accounts Receivable Invoices

Annuities

Auto Notes

Bankruptcy Receivables

Business Notes

Cemetery Pre-Need Contracts

Commercial Deficiency Portfolios

Consumer Deficiency Portfolios

Commercial Judgments

Commercial Leases

Commissions

Consumer Judgments

Credit Card Debt/Charge–offs; Contracts (of any type)

Delinquent Debt

Funeral Purchase Assignments

General Consumer Debt

Health and Country Club Memberships

Equipment Leases

Inheritances

Leases

Lottery Winnings

Mobile Home Notes

Notes on Collectibles

 Equipment Notes

Partnership Agreements

 Student Loans

Residential Lease Payments

Retail Installment Contracts

Royalty Payments

RV Motor Home Notes

Sports Contracts

Tax Liens and Tax Certificates

Tax Refunds

Time Shares and Vacation Club Memberships

Trust Advances

Unsecured Non Performing or Delinquent Debt

Warehouse Inventory Liens

Workers Compensation Awards

Yacht Notes

Request For Quote

Seasoned First Note

Property Location (Street Address)_____

City:_____ State: _____ Zip: _____

Type: SFR _____ 2-4 _____ 5+ _____ SW w/land _____ DW w/land _____ Other _____

OCCUPANCY OO _____ NOO _____

APPRAISED VALUE $ _____DATE _____ESTIMATE_____

Amount of Underlying Liens on Property $_____

If property seller has owned property for less than 12 months:

Acquisition Date: _____ Acquisition Price: _____

PAYER:

Credit Score(s)_____ Estimate: _____ Actual: _____

Down Payment Amount $_____Seasoned _____Non-Seasoned _____

Income Full Doc _____ Stated _____ Debt to Income <50%? Yes _____ No _____

STRUCTURE OF UNDERLYING SALE

      $ _____ Down Payment

      $ _____ Seller-Held First Mortgage

      $ _____ Seller-Held Second Mortgage

$ _____ Sale Price

DETAILS ON FIRST NOTE THAT IS FOR SALE

      Interest Rate: _____ First Payment Date: _____

      Months Amortized Over: _____ Next Payment Due: _____

      Months Due In _____ #Payments Made _____

      Current Balance if known: $ _____

PAYMENT DOCUMENTATION

All Payments Timely: Yes _____ No _____

INDIVIDUAL REQUESTING QUOTE

Name: _____ Telephone: _____

Fax: _____ Relationship To: Dealer____ Broker _____

Property _____ Seller _____ Property Buyer _____

Request For Quote
Simultaneous Closing

PROPERTY

Location (Street Address):_____

City:_____ State: _____ Zip: _____

Type: SFR _____ 2-4 _____ 5+ _____ SW w/land _____ DW w/land _____ Other _____

OCCUPANCY OO _____ NOO _____

APPRAISED VALUE $ _____ DATE _____ ESTIMATE_____

Amount of Underlying Liens on Property $_____

If property seller has owned property for less than 12 months:

Acquisition Date: _____ Acquisition Price: _____

PAYER:

Credit Score(s)_____ Estimate: _____ Actual: _____

Down Payment Amount $_____ Seasoned _____ Non-Seasoned _____

Income Full Doc _____ Stated _____ Debt to Income <50%? Yes ____ No ____

STRUCTURE OF UNDERLYING SALE

    $ _____ Down Payment

    $ _____ Seller-Held First Mortgage

    $ _____ Seller-Held Second Mortgage

$ _____ Sale Price

INDIVIDUAL REQUESTING QUOTE

Name: _____ Telephone: _____

Fax: _____

Relationship To: Dealer____ Broker _____ Property _____ Seller _____

Property Buyer _____

Existing Note Worksheet

Your Name: _____

Phone: _____ Cell: _____ Fax: _____

Company: _____

SALE INFORMATION: Buyer: _____

Pays (Seller): _____

Down Payment: $_____ **Buyers Credit: A B C D**

Sale Price: $_____ 1st Lien _____ 2nd Lien _____

MORTGAGE/TRUST DEED INFORMATION:

	First Lien	*Second Lien*
Date of Mortgage	_____	_____
Original Loan Amount	_____	_____
Term in Months	_____	_____
Interest Rate (%)	_____	_____
Payment Amount	_____	_____
Balloon Date	_____	_____
Balloon Amount	_____	_____
Date First Payment Made	_____	_____
Date Next Payment Due	_____	_____
# of Payments Made	_____	_____
# of Payments Remaining	_____	_____
Current Balance	_____	_____

PROPERTY INFORMATION:

Type (please check one): SFH _____ 2-4 _____ Condo/Townhome: _____

Land _____ Improved Land _____ Mobile Home _____

Owner Occupied (please check one): Yes _____ No_____ (held for rental)

Monthly Rental Income: $ _____

Location (Street Address):_____

City:_____ State: _____ Zip: _____

SELLER NEEDS: $ _____ BROKER NEEDS: $ _____

COMMENTS: _____

_____

_____

_____

_____

_____

_____

Note Purchase Data Sheet

The processing of your note can be expedited by completing the following form in its entirely. Incomplete forms cause delays.

Seller name: _____

(if married, list spouse's name also — information is needed for document preparation)

Street Address: _____

City:_____ State: _____ Zip: _____

Work Phone #: _____ Home Phone # _____

(Note: social security numbers are needed for the preparation of closing documents prior to actual closing)

PAYER INFORMATION

If husband and wife are referenced on the note, then complete information is needed on both in the above spaces provided. <u>This information is a very important part of the total package</u>.

Payer Name: _____ Payer SS#: _____

Home Phone: _____ Cell Phone: _____

Employer: _____Yrs w/ Employer: _____

Work Phone: _____

Spouse Name: _____ Payer SS#: _____

Home Phone: _____ Cell Phone: _____

Employer: _____Yrs w/ Employer: _____

Work Phone: _____

Property:

Street Address: _____

City:_____ State: _____ Zip: _____

If address of payer is different than the address of the property, please list address, city, state above.

PROPERTY CHARACTERISTICS

Size of Lot/Acreage: _____

Type of Structure: (House, Mobile Home, etc.)_____

Square Feet: _____

DOCUMENT CHECKLIST - PLEASE PROVIDE THE FOLLOWING DOCUMENTS

The following is a closing checklist of the items needed to process the purchase of your real estate note:

Payment History On Note (copies of deposit slips, checks, etc.)

Copy of the Current Hazard Insurance Binder

Color Photo of the Property

Location Map

Copy of **Recorded** Mortgage or **Recorded** Deed of Trust

Copy of **Signed** Real Estate Lien Note

Copy of **Signed** Closing Statement

Copy of Mobile Home Title (If Applicable)

Copy of Mortgagee Title Policy insurance

Copy of Credit Application (If Applicable)

AGREEMENT TO BROKER INSTRUMENT (S) KNOWN AS:

NOTE/MORTGAGE _____ NOTE/TRUST DEED _____CONTRACT OR AGREEMENT
(Hereinafter referred to as Instrument)

1. PARTIES: The parties are: (Seller/Assignor) of (address):

(Street)_____

City: _____ State: _____ Zip Code: _____ Phone:

_____ and Buyers: herein declaring that no agency of fiduciary

exists between any of the parties for profit and therefore the parties agree to the following

terms and conditions.

2. TERMS: Seller is the owner (payee or current assignee) of the following described

Instrument (a true and accurate copy of which is attached hereto and referenced as exhibit

"A") and has made no prior transfers, assignments or conveyances of all or any portion of

this Instrument:

DATED: _____ Original Principal Balance: $ _____

Payer: _____ Interest Rate: _____Terms: _____

Payments: _____ Balance: _____

There are _____ payments of remaining plus a balloon of $ _____

Street Address: _____

City:_____ State: _____ Zip: _____

Legal Description: _____

_____

_____

_____

_____

3. AMOUNTS: Seller agrees to sell and broker agrees to use his or her best efforts to find a
   Buyer for said Instrument for the sum of: $_____ payable upon written, ac-
   ceptable clearance by title insurance company, subject to adjustment if the balances,
   terms, payments or conditions stated in paragraph 2 hereto are inaccurate. Pursuant to this
   agreement Seller shall sell payments of _____ beginning
   _____ plus a final balloon payment of $_____ due and
   payable on _____, if consisting of appraisal, title insurance,

credit report, recording fees and courier services. Seller's estimated transaction costs are estimated as follows:

1. Brokerage fee: $_____
2. Closing Costs: $_____
3. Total Transaction Costs: $_____
4. Estimated amount due Seller after all expenses $_____

4. TIMING AND RELEASE: Broker shall have ninety (90) days from this date to secure a commitment from a bona fide Buyer. At closing Seller agrees to execute an assignment of the Instrument and to endorse and deliver the Instrument to the Buyer. If for any reason the Seller does not execute the assignment to Buyer upon demand, or if for any reason Seller withdraws from this agreement, or if for any reason the Seller fails to endorse and deliver the original Instrument to Buyer and/or fails to deliver other original Instruments to Buyer, or if Seller sells this Instrument within twelve (12) months next after the termination of this Brokerage Agreement to a buyer whom Buyer submitted said Instrument for sale during the term of this agreement then seller agrees to pay and authorizes to be paid to broker an amount of money equal to six (6%) percent of the outstanding balance as of this date plus all incurred costs such as legal fees, appraisals, credit checks, title insurance, processing fee, etc., plus all reasonable attorney fees. Any conflicts between parties herein shall be decided in the court and location chosen solely by the Broker.

5. TITLE: Seller warrants that his interest as owner (current assignee) in the real property which is the subject matter of the above described Instrument is marketable and insurable. If a title examination reveals that it is not marketable or insurable, Seller agrees to exercise diligent and reasonable efforts to render his interest marketable and insurable or Buyer, at his option, may do the same at Seller's expense.

6. WARRANTS: Seller warrants that the above described Instrument has not been obtained or created in any fashion which violates any state, federal or local laws, that there are no legal or equitable defenses or offsets to the payment of said Instrument, that there have been no amendments, modification, extensions or addendums of any kind, and that as of this date there is no default of any kind in the Instrument. Seller shall further indemnify and hold harmless Buyer from any and all liability, loss or damage Seller may suffer as a

result of any claims, demands, costs or judgments which may result from the representations and warranties herein made being untrue. Finally, Seller warrants that there are no restrictions against assignment of this note.

7. DOCUMENTS: Seller agrees to provide all documents and information which may be reasonably required by the Buyer to determine the Seller's interest in the property, the value of the property and the reliability of the payer. Seller authorizes buyer and/or its assigns to obtain any/all credit information on payers, including but not limited to using credit reporting agencies and references. Seller warrants that he shall hold broker harmless and absolutely defend broker from all claims arising from such inquiries and information.

8. LAWS: This agreement shall be construed in all respects in accordance with the laws and decisions of the state of _____. Typewritten provisions inserted herein or attached hereto as addenda shall control all provisions in conflict herewith.

9. ADDITIONAL AGREEMENTS: _____

_____

_____

_____

_____

_____

_____

_____

TIME IS OF THE ESSENCE. THIS IS A BINDING AGREEMENT. SEEK LEGAL ADVICE IF NOT FULLY UNDERSTOOD.

Required Document Checklist

SIMULTANEOUS RESIDENTIAL LOAN:

Please include all items indicated with an "X".

Req'd	Required Documents/Information
X	Signed Contract with Note Company
X	Note Submission Worksheet (attached)
	Borrower Information/Pay History Form (attached)
	Authorization to Release Information (attached)
X	Copy of Proposed Promissory Note
X	Copy of Proposed Mortgage/Deed of Trust/Contract for Deed
	Copy of Settlement Statement/Closing Statement
X	Copy of Existing Title Policy/Title commitment
X	Copy of Current Hazard Insurance Binder/Evidence of Insurance
X	Current Photo of the Property (may be e-mailed)
X	Copy of Most Recent Appraisal if any (do not order new appraisal)
	If Mobile Home, need Mobile Home Title & Certificate of Attachment
	If Note Seller is a Corporation, Need Articles of Inc. & Corp. Resolution
	In Underlying Mortgage to be paid at closing, Need Payoff Letter from Bank
	If sale result of Trust or Probate, Need Trust and/or Probate Docs.
X	Copy of Purchase & Sale Agreement
X	Copy of 1003 Credit Application Signed by Borrower
X	Proof of Down Payment
	Commercial Questionnaire
	Rent Roll (if applicable)
	12 months Operating Statement
	Two Years Tax Returns
	Three Years Corporate Financial Statements
	EPA Report

We realize that some of the above requested documents may not be available to the Note Seller and/or may not be applicable.

Please call us if you have any questions regarding the above referenced documents.

Often times, we can research documents on your behalf or, in some cases, can make an exception to the required documents depending on the rest of the file.

It is important that you send as much of the above referenced documents as soon as possible so that we may expedite the processing of your transaction.

Should you have any questions, please call.

Thank you for returning our initial request for information that kicked off the final stage of underwriting on your file. Once again, we appreciate the decision you and/or your broker have made to place your trust in us.

Based on the information that you provided, we have the following Open Underwriting Requirements.

❑ <u>Timing of Closing</u> — Please confirm the desires of you and your buyer to close in the _____ month of _____; the transaction could have relevant '_____ income ramifications for you as seller.

❑ <u>Title</u> — Lenders Title Commitment, showing the current Title holder as the proposed insured (lender is the current owner, as this is a seller carry-back mortgage that is being sold).

❑ <u>Collateral financials</u> — 1) two fiscal years of financials OR MAI commercial appraisal that reflects income approach and 2) copies of all leases in place.

❑ <u>Payer Income</u> — Description of documentation available (final determination of extent of need will be related to property financial information).

❑ <u>1003</u> — Revised 1003 that reflects source of 10% down payment.

❑ <u>Escrow Account Monies</u> — Please confirm that buyer is aware that down payment must pass through escrow account (i.e. copy of cashiers check or equivalent to be provided by closing agent at close).

❑ <u>Underlying payoffs</u> — Please confirm that there is no underlying mortgage AND provide estimate of all other items that must be satisfied prior to final Title Policy (ex. Taxes due within next 30 days, etc.).

Seller Follow-up

House Buyer: _____

Your Name: _____

Type of Deal: SIMO _____ CI _____ Existing $_____

Date of Offer Presented to Seller: _____ Full _____ Partial _____

No. Pmts. of $_____ $_____ of

Balloon For $_____ (your pay price)

Seller comments about offer: _____

_____

_____

_____

_____

IF DEAL IS ACCEPTED, PLEASE FILL OUT THE INFORMATION BELOW

Seller Acceptance Date: _____

Seller Name: _____

Street Address: _____

City:_____ State: _____ Zip: _____

Amount of Seller: $_____ Amount to Broker: $_____

Property Street Address: _____

City:_____ State: _____ Zip: _____

Comments: _____

_____

_____

_____

_____

THIS FORM SHOULD BE FAXED BACK WITHIN 72 HOURS

Note: This is offered with no representation or warranties. Consult an attorney familiar with the laws of your state before using this contract.

Co-Broker Agreement

Date: _____

It is mutually agreed that _____
are principal client(s) of _____
hereafter referred to as "Remitting broker." Remitting Broker in its efforts to secure a mortgage loan, mortgage commitment and/or mortgage sale for the above client(s) in the amount
of $ _____ did contact _____
herein referred to as the "Accepting Broker." Accepting Broker does hereby agree to exert its
best efforts to obtain a commitment for the above client(s).

Accepting Broker agrees to pay remitting Broker _____ percent (%) of the mortgage
loan amount/mortgage(s), note(s) sale/purchase price. The total loan amount/sale/ purchase
amount is to be listed by agreement/contract, provided that the Accepting Broker has obtained a written commitment.

Remitting Broker agrees to the amount of fee provided that said requested commitment has
been secured by Accepting Broker by (date) _____. It is further agreed that
the Accepting Broker will supply the Remitting Broker with copies of the commitment and
the necessary closing documents upon closing in order that both

Remitting Broker and Accepting Broker be in compliance with applicable State and/or
Federal Statutes. It is mutually understood a state of non-circumvention shall apply to all
clients and lenders/buyers for a period of _____ (_____) years, unless permission is given and accepted in writing by both parties to nullify this covenant.

Name: _____

Name: _____

Co-Broker Agreement continued….

Remitting Broker's Signature: _____

Accepting Broker's Signature: _____

Broker's Title: _____

Broker's Title: _____

Broker's License No.: _____

State of: _____

Broker License No.: _____

State of: _____

Credit Report Authorization Letter

Date: _____

To: _____ (Any credit reporting agency)

To enable (Seller)_____ to make a final decision concerning the sale of their property to us on terms, we are providing our social security numbers and authorize you to issue the Sellers a Credit Report on us.

Name of Buyer (#1): _____

Social Security Number: _____

Current Home Street Address:_____

City, State, Zip: _____

Home Phone:_____ Cell Phone:_____

Work Phone: _____

Previous Home Address (within the last five years):

Street Address:_____

City, State, Zip: _____

Current employer: _____

Street Address: _____

City, State, Zip: _____ Phone: _____

Date: _____ **Signature**: _____

Name of Buyer (#2): _____

Social Security Number: _____

Current Home Street Address:_____

City, State, Zip: _____

Home Phone:_____ Cell Phone:_____

Work Phone: _____

Buyer (#2):

Previous Home Address (within the last five years):

Street Address:_____

City, State, Zip: _____

Current employer: _____

Street Address: _____

City, State, Zip: _____ Phone: _____

Date: _____ **Signature**: _____

Index

BOOKS, COURSES

and

SEMINARS

By

E. Wright Davis

Getting Started in Creative Real Estate Investing

Book by E. Wright Davis

Learn 21 of the most creative real estate investing techniques ever known.

This is the only manual you will ever need when it comes to creative real estate investing and finance. Most of the techniques taught utilize owner financing and very little conventional bank financing.

Some of the techniques you will learn from this book including forms and examples of typical contract clauses:

√ Cash to existing mortgage.

√ Paper out offer.

√ Seller refinance with a first mortgage crank.

√ Seller refinance with a second mortgage crank.

√ Created paper down payment.

√ Paper out offer subject to seller trading paper.

√ Blanket mortgage combined with a second mortgage crank.

√ Lease with option to purchase.

√ Reverse interest loan offer.

√ Paper used as substituted collateral

√ Contract clauses, forms and techniques to pay off your mortgage fast.

√ MANY more techniques.

Cost: $39 (plus shipping and handling)

How to Crack the Mortgage Code -
The 19 Greatest Ways To Pay Off Your Mortgage Fast

by E. Wright Davis

In this Course Package, you will receive:

1. A complete workbook/manual with forms

2. A 2-hour DVD live presentation on how to utilize the 19 techniques

You will learn:

√ How to save hundreds of thousands of dollars in unnecessary interest payments.

√ How to reduce the payoff period of a mortgage from 30 years to 5-10 years.

√ How to stop foreclosures cold.

√ The 8 mortgage myths.

√ The secrets behind the time value of money principles.

√ How to create a cash flow machine from real estate.

Cost: $69 (plus shipping and handling)

Calculator Power

By Jon Richards and David Roberts
Course by E. Wright Davis
(Included as a BONUS in the seminar package)

This manual and the accompanying FREE DVD's will give you all the hands on step-by-step instruction on every aspect of the operation of the financial calculator you will ever need.

This is a full 8-hour course with comprehensive easy to understand instructions.

With this course, you will learn how to:

√ Structure offers to buy real estate notes.

√ Structure real estate financing utilizing the concepts of the time value of money.

√ Calculate payments on a loan.

√ Calculate the remaining balance due on a mortgage.

√ Calculate balloon payments.

√ Calculate the time value of money concepts.

√ Calculate the present value of streams of real estate income.

√ Discount real estate income to present value.

√ Make offers that will insure more closing utilizing these concepts.

Cost: $249 Plus shipping and handling.

To Place Your Book Order

On the internet or by phone:

Information for ordering E. Wright Davis's books on the internet or by phone
using a credit card or PayPal can be found at:

www.ewrightdavis.com

Viewing Live Streaming Seminars & Webinars
via the internet

To view live streaming seminars and/or webinars via the internet, complete instructions
to sign up with details regarding dates, times and registration fees can be found at:

www.ewrightdavis.com

Attending E. Wright Davis's Live Seminars in person:

To attend one of E. Wright Davis's live seminars in person, complete details regarding
location, dates, times and registration fees can be found at:

www.ewrightdavis.com

www.ingramcontent.com/pod-product-compliance
Lightning Source LLC
Chambersburg PA
CBHW080543220326

41599CB00032B/6346